How to Win
The War Within
and Discover Your
Purpose for Living

A Short Journal to Guide Your Eternal Destiny

Part One of a Three-Part Series

By

Brian "The Watchman" Arnold, NHM

ISBN: 978 0 9986451 93

Copyright 2017 by Brian Arnold

Printed in the U. S. A.

Library of Congress Number: 2017957639

Layout and Design by Pizzirani Consulting

How to Win the War Within and Discover Your Purpose for Living

A Short Journal to Guide Your Eternal Destiny

Name

Date

A Gift From

Matthew 6:33 Seek first the Kingdom of God
and His Righteousness and all these things
(you have need of) shall be added unto you.

Table of Contents

Questionnaire

- Are you fearful of what is coming upon the Earth right now?
- **Do you struggle with fear, uncertainty and doubt?**
- Are you stressed, weary, confused, tired, and worn out?
- **Are you sick and tired of feeling sick and tired?**
- Are you suffering from a broken-heart and seeking inner healing?
- **Do you feel frustrated at times with your job, your life, or your relationships?**
- Are you worried about your future, your family or a child?
- **Do you feel battered, bruised, down and out...even suicidal?**
- Are you struggling to know your purpose for being here on planet Earth?
- **Do you feel powerless at times to overcome obstacles?**
- Do you feel hatred, anger, resentment or retaliation toward another?
- **Do you struggle with sadness, hopelessness or depression?**

If you answered "YES" to any of the above questions...cheer-up...I have some "good news" for you!

The good news is...you can renew your mind and be TRANSFORMED inwardly through this powerful E-L-E-C-T-R-I-F-Y-I-N-G little journal and find out...

- **Who you are (Identity)**
- Why you're here (Purpose)
- **Where you're from (Origins)...and...**
- Where you are going (Your Final Destiny Through Choices)

Notes, Thoughts, Ideas

Observations, things I want to Change in my life...and
new understandings.

What This Little Journal "Is NOT" About

It is NOT about man-made religions of the world.

It is NOT a religion.

It is NOT about Evolution, the Illuminati, philosophy, theory, trilateral Commission, UFO's, Jehovah Witnesses, Mormonism, Communism, Buddhism, Socialism, Capitalism, Confucianism, Taoism, Sikhism, Zoroastrianism, Agnosticism, Shintoism, Shamanism, Atheism, New Age spiritualism or any other "ism"...including Catholicism and all its Protestantism "religious denominations and daughters". It is NOT about Islam, Allah nor Mohammad. It is NOT about Baha'i, Reincarnation, Idol worship, or any other "man-made belief" reaching toward heaven to find the One True Almighty Creator of the Universe, Universal Laws and man's existence for being here on planet earth and how we got here.

What This Little Journal "IS" About.

This little journal is about two powerful invisible Kingdoms at war within you. The Kingdom of darkness, depression, death and destruction (the first Adam's **"fallen race"**)...and The Kingdom of light, life, love, and freedom (the second Adam, Jesus Christ's, **"resurrected race"**). They are at war for Your soul and Your mind is the battleground. You choose who wins. Which "race" are you in? **"The fallen" or "the resurrected"?** There is no "third race of religion".

There's a story about an old Cree Indian. His name was Harry. The story goes that an old friend of Harry's asked him one day, "How are you doing, Harry?" Old Harry thought for a bit, then replied, "Well, I feel like I have a raging war going on inside of me." "What do you mean," asked his friend. "Well," said Harry, "I feel like I have two big dogs fighting inside of me. A big black dog of darkness and despair and a big white dog of winning and hope."

"Well, which one is winning," asked his friend, and Old Harry in his simplicity replied, "whichever one I feed the most!" The truth of the matter is we all have...**Two Dogs Fighting Within Us.** The question is: Which dog are you feeding the most? 97% of all news media, movies and video games feed the black dog deceptive murderous "bad news". This little journal feeds the spiritual white dog the "good news" of the Kingdom of God within you. Which one will you feed the most?

Choosing your Destiny over Suicide

How to Overcome Fear, Uncertainty, Doubt, Depression, Suicidal Thoughts and Self Destruction!

According to Emory University, "The rate of suicide is between .5 and 7.5 per 100,000 among college students. There are more than 1,000 suicides on college campuses per year. That's 3 a day! Suicide is the second-leading cause of death among people aged 25-34 and the third-leading cause of death among people aged 15-24". How tragic. How sad. How shocking. Yet it's true!

Here are a few facts about Suicide in the United States

- Emory University goes on to say, "Each year, 34,598 people die by suicide, an average of 94 completed suicides every day! That's more than the horrific tragedy of the Las Vegas shooting rampage happening privately every single day! This insanity must be stopped! But how? The answer is in this little journal.
- **More people die by suicide 34,598, than by homicide (18,361) in the U.S. alone!**
- Suicide is the eleventh-leading cause of death across all ages.
- **Fifty-four percent of completed suicides are done by firearms.**
- Every year 864,950 people attempt suicide, which means 1 person attempts suicide every 38 seconds! Could this be your child, grandchild or someone you know and care about?
- **More than 395,000 people are treated in emergency rooms every year for self-inflicted injuries. That's more than 1000 attempted**

**suicides every day. That's more every day than
the horrific Las Vegas rampage...every day!**

- 1 in 10 college students have made a plan for
suicide. What's going on in the heart of humanity?

More facts about Depression and Suicide

Depression is a common "mental health disorder" (Dis-order, or out of order thinking, or not thinking right).

- **Two thirds of people that die by suicide are
depressed at the time of their death.**
- Among those that have major depression, the risk of
death by suicide is 20 times greater than those that
are not depressed.
- **Unwillingness to seek help is another risk factor
for suicide.**

Risk Factors for Suicide according to Emory

1. Depression
2. Hopelessness
3. Anxiety
4. Isolation or lack of social support
5. Alcohol and or substance abuse
6. Loss (in relationship, socially, financially or work
related)
7. Previous suicide attempts
8. Family history of suicide
9. Family history of maltreatment
10. History of mental disorders (dis-order or wrong
thinking)
11. Access to lethal means
12. Unwillingness to seek help.

Risk Factors Specific to College Students

1. New environment
2. Loss of social network
3. Loss of safety net found at home
4. Pressure academically or socially (peer pressure)
5. Isolation and alienation
6. Lack of coping skills
7. It is said, 90% of people who attempt suicide, survive, but could try again and that someone we love dies by suicide every 11.9 minutes.

By the time you read this page in 2 minutes...10 people will have taken their lives in Canada and the United States!

Over 50% of the entire population of Canada and The United States has been touched and scared within their soul by the self-destruction of suicide of a family member...and...it is this authors intention to bring healing to these scars and hope to the hopeless.

I have some good news for you.

Very good news!

And...it's not about false man-made religions.

It worked for me...and...it will work for anyone battling "mental disorders, depression and hopelessness!" I was just seconds away from pulling the trigger...and...I had a divine intervention.

To read my short story of how I passed from the Kingdom of Darkness, suicidal thoughts, death and self-destruction into the Kingdom of Light, hope and purpose... INSTANTLY... go to the back of this journal. **The main purpose for this little journal is not only for eternal guidance for you "the reader" but for you to reach out to those around you struggling with depression...and...give them one of these journals.**

The #1 reason for suicide is "depression". The meaning of depression is "feelings of severe despondency, dejection, self-doubt, and hopelessness".

One of the main reason for depression and hopelessness is **"lack of purpose"** and understanding for the "reason why" a person is here on planet earth at this time.

"Depression" is a part of the "Kingdom of Darkness" within you.

"Purpose" for "living" is a part of the "Kingdom of Light" within you.

So then, in order to overcome "depression" you must have a **"purpose"** for being.

You must first **"be"** before you can **"do"** and you can **"do"** only to the extent that you **"are"** and what you **"are"** depends upon what you **"think"** for "as a man thinks in his heart, so is **he**".

My objective for this first 30-day course is for you (every individual) to **find your purpose** for being here on planet earth at this exact time in history. My purpose, my vision, my mission, and my calling is to bring you this "good news" of the "Kingdom of God" within you...without being religious.

This Little Journal is Designed To...

- Give hope to the hopeless, help to the helpless, inner healing to the broken hearted, deliverance to those taken captive in addictions, inner vision to those blinded to Truth, and eternal life to those lost and contemplating self-destruction, or suicide.
- The reason for this short little spiritual journal is not to overwhelm you but to help you understand the simplicity of the "Kingdom of God" in small bite-size pieces that you can spiritually eat daily...and be

12

TRANSFORMED within. This inner **transformation** comes by renewing your mind to the Word of God.

-

Sincerely...Your Friend

Brian "The Watchman" Arnold NHM.

Notes, Thoughts, Ideas

Observations, things I want to Change in my life...and new understandings.

Rediscovering The "Kingdom of God Within You"

To start out on your journey in this journal you must first understand who you are, your purpose for being here, how you got here and...where you are going based on your decisions. You must also understand the mind of God "The Almighty Creator" of the heavens, the earth, universal laws such as the law of gravity, the law of physics, the law of mathematics and all the laws that govern His Kingdom.

These laws are exact. If you break a law the law breaks you. These laws were set into motion by the "Word of God." **Walk in righteousness not lawlessness**.

God's word is God's will, for He wouldn't will one thing and say or write another. So God's Word "The Bible" is NOT a religious book but a book of God's Word and serves as an instruction manual for successful living in God's Kingdom. God wrote the Bible through several different secretaries over 1500 years. In short...the Bible is a legal document which contains the contract for eternal life in a Kingdom for its citizens. It's like the constitution of the United States of America for its citizens.

Ideas are the most powerful invisible "brain child" man can have. Invisible thoughts and concepts can be crystallized into reality through meditation on these thoughts. The Bible is God's thoughts and words as a guide to your eternal destiny.

Concepts are Produced by Ideas

God's Word "The Bible" is God's concept of His Kingdom. God's Word is God's Will that he speaks to us and we must understand His concept of His Kingdom through His Word. The word "religion" means "to search." All religions are searching for truth. Jesus said, I am the way, **The Truth** and the life and no one comes to the Father but by me. Jesus is the door…and the way…into the "Kingdom of God" that all religions are searching for but never finding. **GOD'S WORD** is **TRUTH AND ALWAYS FINAL AUTHORITY!**

It is critical that we get the right "concept" of God's Kingdom or we fall into "mis-conception". Misconception leads to false religions, false beliefs, deceptions, and deadly error resulting in eternal damnation rather than eternal life!

"Concepts" are the source of communication that determines our understanding and final outcome. If your **"concept"** is wrong then your **"conclusions"** will be wrong with the final result being **"misconception"** and eternal separation from God.

Therefore, we must get the **"right concept"** of God's idea, plan and purpose for "His Kingdom" to be set up here on earth.

That's why we need right knowledge, right thinking, right understanding and use God's wisdom and insights to walk in His Kingdom and NOT in man-made religions!

God's word is always final authority. Jesus declared' in Matthew 4:4 "Man shall not live by bread alone, but by every word that proceeds out of the mouth of God."

The heart of Jesus' teachings centers around the theme of the "Kingdom of God" or the "Kingdom of Heaven".

John, the Baptist, introduced Christ to the world declaring; **"Repent for the "Kingdom of Heaven" is at hand."**

Matthew 4:17 From that time Jesus began to preach, and to say, **"repent for the Kingdom of Heaven is at hand".**

Mark 1:15 Jesus saying, "The time is fulfilled and the "Kingdom of God" is at hand; Repent ye and believe the gospel."

Matthew 24:14 And **THIS GOSPEL OF THE "KINGDOM"** (not some religious man-made religion) will be proclaimed throughout the whole world as a testimony to all nations, and **THEN** will the end come.

What is "The Kingdom of God" Concept?

God never originally intended to have any religion but rather...to establish "His Kingdom on Earth." God's mission statement is found in Genesis 1: 26, 27 & 28.

26) And God said, let us make man in our image, after our likeness (a creative mirror of himself) and let them have dominion over the fish of the sea, and over the fowl of the air, and over the cattle and over all the earth, and over every creeping thing that creeps upon the earth (including our cats, dogs, horses and pets).

27) So God created man in his own image, (a mirror of himself, an invisible spirit being) in the image of God created he him; male and female created he them.

28) And God blessed them and God said unto them, be fruitful, and multiply, and replenish the earth, and subdue it; and have dominion over the fish of the sea, and over the fowl of the air, and over every living thing that moves upon the earth.

God's First Assignment to Man

The word "dominion" in the Hebrew is "radah", meaning, to reign and rule over. To subdue, to tread down as a wine press with the feet.

In other words, man is here to manage, control, have dominion or dominate, or manage and have stewardship of the resources of God's creation. God gave man authority and

17

rulership and responsibility not to dominate and rule over others...but to rule over the resources (your finances to further his Kingdom), look after and take care of "the earth." God gave the first Adam a "Kingdom" (not a religion) to rule and reign over.

When the first man Adam fell in the garden of Eden through disobedience, he did not lose a religion...he lost a "Kingdom". He turned his dominion over to Satan and Satan became the ruler over this earth. Satan became the "god of this world".

The Kingdom of God is more than salvation or the church; it is God manifesting himself through His Believers "his body" here on earth.

In John 14:23 Jesus said, "If a man love me, he will keep my words: and my Father will love him, and we will make our abode (mansion, habitation) with him. God will live "in you" through Christ...if you will abide or live in His word and seek after him. This is how you "Win The War Within".

So God is beginning His spiritual rule and Kingdom on earth in the hearts of and among his people. We don't have a gun, drug, or alcohol problem. We have a "HEART" problem! Guns don't kill people...it's the wicked heart that causes the finger to squeeze the trigger.

The Kingdom of God is not a religious-political theocracy; The world, at present, and its Anti-Christ system, its world leaders, and Satan's Kingdom of darkness remain at war and an enemy of God and his body of believers. God's rule by direct judgement and force will come into full force at the end of this age at the battle of Armageddon and Christs second return.

In summary... The "Kingdom of God" has both a present (salvation within our hearts) and a future (setting up of the "Kingdom of God") on earth with Christ ruling through His body..."you and me!"

The work and influence of Satan and evil, and his corrupt, greedy people will continue until the end of this age...which is soon to end, by the signs of the times.

The ultimate fulfillment of the "Kingdom of God" comes when Christ finally triumphs over all evil...including death...and hands over the Kingdom to God, The Father.

This is the "good news" of the "gospel" that Jesus preached...anything less results in error, delusion, disappointment, and backsliding back into the world and perishing for lack of "right concept knowledge" about God's Kingdom and His righteousness!

Notes, Thoughts, Ideas

Observations, things I want to Change in my life...and new understandings.

The 4 Key Questions
That Control the World

These 4 key questions asked by the hordes of humanity demand answers. They create industry, entertainment, fashion, the US constitution, our laws, control our destinies, economics and our futures!

Here are the 4 key questions and we shall answer each one specifically to clarify your questions, overcome depression and empower you to empower others!

1. **Who am I? (Identity)**
2. Where am I from? (What is my source? Not ethnic, heritage, or country)
3. **Why am I here? (Purpose)**
4. Where am I going? (Destiny, life after death?)

Let's begin with question #1.

Who Am I? (Identity)

1. You are a three-part being "in-one" (spirit, soul and body) You are a spirit being from the invisible realm of heaven manifesting in the natural realm of earth. Your outward manifestation has its origins from within. In other words the "Kingdom of God" and the "Kingdom of Satan" are both invisible spiritual forces warring "within you" for your soul and manifesting outwardly through your actions. This is the knowledge of the Tree of good and evil.

2. **You are a spirit being. You have a soul (your mind, emotions and will) ...and...you live in a physical body with five senses.**

3. Your outer body is formed from the dust (humas) of the ground and has five senses.
    A. Sight

21

    B. Touch

    C. Smell

    D. Taste

    E. Hearing

4. **A. Feelings are the "voice" of your "body"**
   B. Reasoning is the "voice" of your "soul"
   C. Conscience is the "voice" of your "spirit"

5. Your brain is an organ of your body taking in all your surroundings through your nervous system connected to your five physical senses sight, touch, smell, taste, and hearing. This makes you "world conscious."

6. **Your soul is your...**
   A. Mind
   B. Emotions
   C. Will

   (More on these 3 and their functions in Part Two of this Three-part series)

7. Your mind is "an organ" of your soul, linked to your spirit, like your brain is an organ to your body linked to your five senses. Your soul is the mediator between your outer body (outward conscious) and your inner spirit man. (The real you).

8. **Your mind is the battleground of the "Kingdom of darkness" at war with the "Kingdom of Light" within you. This war within you is for your soul and your eternal destiny through your choices.**

9. Thoughts are invisible spiritual seeds (good or evil) sown into your mind through news media, TV, internet, music, violent games, movies, music,

friends, schools, university, books and other mediums.

Note: Media is a part of "mediums".

Medium, according to Webster's dictionary, means: "The intervening substance through which impressions are conveyed to the "senses" (your 5 senses) or a "force" (life or death) acts on an object from a distance. Eg. Radio, TV, etc. Meaning "the middle, midst, center," or "getting into your spirit, the heart, or "the real you!" Satan "the god of this world" is also known as the "prince of the power of the air"...waves. **Note:** There is only **One Mediator** between God and man, the man Christ Jesus. 1 Timothy 2:5

Recent Studies have revealed the average child watches 28 hours of TV, internet and violent games...weekly. By the age of 18 they have seen over 20,000 murders on TV and movies and 200,000 hours of violence. The tragic massacre of Las Vegas was not the guns but the heart...influenced by darkness of Satan's media, Hollywood, and an evil, wicked heart! Protect your eyes and ears!

10. **Your Inner Spirit "The Real You"**
    A. **Your "Breath of Life"**
    B. **The real you**
    C. **The hidden man of the heart**
    D. **Your inner core being**

In Summary: you are not your body. The real you will never die. You are a spirit being. Your origins are from God. You were created in His image and likeness. God is Spirit. You mirror God as a creative spirit being, you have a soul (mind, emotions and will) and you live in a physical body. You are NOT your body. When your physical body dies and is buried...you are not there. Because you are a spirit being you instantly leave your body and are escorted by angels (depending on your spiritual choice) to your final destination of (Paradise or Hades. Hades is not hell, but a holding area until the **GREAT WHITE THRONE JUDGEMENT**) based on "your choice" today. Luke 16:19-25

Your body is your "natural" physical temple of manifestation while here on earth. When your body dies...you leave...and it's not for purgatory. There's no such place or "second chance". Ecclesiastes 12:7 states: Then shall the dust (your physical body) return to the earth as it was: and the spirit, the **"eternal supernatural"**, shall return unto God who gave it.

Spirit, Soul & Body

1. You are a spirit being
2. You have a soul (mind, emotion & will)
3. You live in a body

Your Soul

-Your mind
-Your emotions
-Your Will

Your mind is
-"An organ of
your spirit"
-It is the battle
ground of good
versus evil
-Thoughts are
spiritual and flow
through your
mind from
your spirit

Outer Body - Physical

Brain: An organ of the
body & the five senses

1. Sight
2. Touch
3. Smell
4. Taste
5. Hearing

Inner Spirit

-Spiritual
-The real you
-The "I AM"
The "Hidden Man
of the Heart"
-Your inner
core being

Feelings are the voice of your body.
Reasoning is the voice of your soul.
Consceince is the the voice of your spirit.

What you think about... you speak about... and what you
speak about... you bring about. Good or evil!
You create the atmosphere you live in
by the thoughts you think upon.

© Arnold Enterprises

25

Notes, Thoughts, Ideas

Observations, things I want to Change in my life...and new understandings.

Why Am I Here?

As it says in Genesis 1:26 "Man is here to have "dominion" or "rulership" over the earth. Not to rule over people, but to rule over the earth and its resources! You are here to lead and to manage in God's Kingdom.

Here are a few facts:

- The key to God's plan to ruling over the earth was given to the male man. This is God's plan...not yours or mine.

- **The male man is not at the top, but at the bottom. He is the foundation of the family.**

- The female or wo-man (woman) is the help mate of the man.

- **The males first priority in life is his work. That's why God placed man in the garden of Eden was to work. To subdue, have rulership, responsibility and management of earth's resources.**

- A woman needs a man's work to succeed because she is highly skilled as man's helpmate.

- **Eve met Adam in God's presence in the garden...working! Managing the earth's resources. Adam named all the bugs, the birds and the animals. An elephant is still an elephant today regardless of what the so called "scientists" call it!**

- Work makes man valuable. A man's work is a man's worth.

- **Man finds his fulfillment in His work.**

- The male man was assigned and given his work before he was given a woman.

- **Man is created and wired to be in control, but not to dominate others...but manage resources of God's earth.**

- In Genesis 1:26 the word "dominion" in the Hebrew text is "Radah"-Kingdom, govern, (government) rule, lead, (leadership) manage, (management) control. Today, because of Adams fall we have "corrupt government." But Jesus is coming to set-up His Kingdom on earth and the "Government" will be upon His shoulders! That's why preaching "His Kingdom" is so important so we can "understand" His concept of ruling and reigning in life.

- **In other words, "To rule, reign, and dominate with the Kingdom culture. (Not a democracy, republic, socialism, communism, capitalism, nor a religion).**

- God's vision, plan, idea, strategy, and goal is to fill the earth with the culture of Heaven. God is King. Man (those reborn into God's Kingdom through Christ) lives in the Royal family of God's Kingdom. God's Kingdom is God's culture.

- **That's why in the Lord's prayer, Jesus prayed "Our Father which art in heaven, hallowed be thy name. Thy Kingdom "come" thy "will" be "done" on "earth"...as it is in "heaven". Jesus prayed for "heaven" to come to "earth". Man's religious ideas have it in reverse and are always preaching about going to Heaven (this is critical!).**

- Man is to occupy, subdue, rule and reign, manage, and govern earth until Jesus' second return. (Not be religious, corrupt, perverted in sin and calling our own shots, shaking our fist at God, worshiping false images and idols, praying to Mary, calling all the Popes over the centuries "Holy Father", and wondering why the world is such a mess!)

- This religious system of Satan's Kingdom will be judged according to Revelation 17:5!

Which Kingdom are you in? The Kingdom of Light or the Kingdom of Darkness?

Which Kingdom are you following? The Kingdom of Darkness or the Kingdom of Light?

Which Kingdom are you supporting with your finances? The Kingdom of darkness, drugs, alcohol and parties, or...the Kingdom of God and winning souls to Christ for eternity?

Notes, Thoughts, Ideas

Observations, things I want to Change in my life...and
new understandings.

Question #3

What's my purpose for being here?

You are here for an assignment. You are extremely valuable as a person. Your job is not your work. Your work assignment is "within you". It's your gift(s) and talent(s).

Here are a few facts:

- The Greek word "work" is Erigon: meaning: to become, to manifest, reveal, to discover through self manifestation, or, self discovery.

- **Your work is your calling in life. Your job is what they pay you to do 8 hours a day. They can fire you from your job, but they can't fire you from your work (your calling) because your work is your assignment, your giftings and talents within you. Your work is to do the works of God in His Kingdom...NOT...the works of Satan and his false religions and deceptions of darkness like Ouija boards, Tea cup readings, man-made religions and astrology or other occult enchantments.**

- Your work is to "become your true self" It's self discovery. We must first "**Be**" before we can "**do**" and we can "**do**" only to the extent that we "**are**" and what we "**are**" depends upon what we "**think**" for as a man "**thinks**" in his heart so is he. Proverbs 23:7

- **What you think about, you speak about, and what you speak about, you bring about. Words are vessels that carry thoughts which manifest into this natural world. Death and life are in the Power of the Tongue. Work is becoming and manifesting your calling in the Kingdom of God on earth as we think and speak it into existence through Christ.**

- The male's priority in life is "work" because it's God's first purpose for why man was created. It was to take care of God's creation.

- **Your work is the source of your purpose and vision.**

- So then the male's purpose is in his work. If man does not work, the female gets frustrated and goes to work on her own.

- **Jesus said, "I come to work the works of God"**

- Proverbs 18:16 states: A man's gift makes room for him, and brings him before great men.

- **Your gift "within you" is your purpose. God placed your gift, your purpose, your vision, your mission, your assignment, and your calling "within you" like a seed "becomes" the tree it was created to be.**

- Your future is trapped "within you"

- **Your reason for "be"ing here is to manifest your gift(s) and talent(s) before you die. You may be a mess right now. Feel like there's no hope. You may have failed 10 times or 100 times or 1000 times. That's your past. We are talking now about your future while living here in the present. You may feel confused. Drugs, alcohol, and addictions may rule and control your life. But...when you decide to surrender your life to Christ...REPENT...from your evil wicked ways...Renew your mind to God's word...which is God's will...you can overcome, have your mission fulfilled and manifest God's greatness in the earth...because you become a part of the Royal Family in the Kingdom of God! Anything less than this...you are in rebellion and on Satan's team and an enemy of God! Meditation**

of your mind won't save your soul on the GREAT
WHITE THRONE JUDGEMENT DAY!

- You have a free will and freedom to choose. If you choose to come up with excuses, listen to losers, propaganda, false teachers, philosophy of man or just flat rebellion against God...your soul is in great danger of eternal separation from God for eternity and headed for hell.

- **Walk away from your past (I did). This is repentance and choosing to walk upright or in righteousness!**

- Walk away from your oppression, and the shadow of failure, depression, suicidal thoughts, a "poor me" victim attitude, which leads to self destruction.

- **Separate yourself from evil, wicked friends, drug addicts, drunks, gamblers, pornography, homosexuality, revelers, evil plotters, and even family and friends, who are ungodly liars that curse God and in rebellion! Save yourself through Christ!** *This is how you win the "War Within".* **It's a fierce war! Satan wants to kill you and take you to hell with him. God loves you and Christ died for you to spend eternity in God's Kingdom. The choice is yours.**

- Come out from under the pain and walk on top of your past. Walk in the "Kingdom of God" in the power of the Holy Spirit.

- **Walk in the freedom of "FOREGIVENESS", washed by the blood of the Lamb of God, "Jesus Christ".**

- Put on the "mind of Christ" and share the "good news" of the Kingdom of God "within you" to others.

- **This is your purpose.**

- Your purpose is to be a problem solver and a soul winner!

- **Every problem is a business or a ministry or an opportunity to help someone and expand the Kingdom of God!**

- You were born to rule, reign, and solve problems while here on planet earth. Not gripe, complain, and expect a corrupt government to take care of you. Get into God's Kingdom and be right...or...you're part of the problem. "Be" the solution. The solution for depression is NOT drugs but purpose.

- **Your value is "within you". Your gift is "within you". You were born to win, but conditioned to lose by the system. The worlds system ruled by the "Kingdom of darkness", depression, sorcery drugs, rebellion, death, and destruction. Satan comes to rob, steal, kill, and destroy your soul, your gift and your calling. Jesus came that you might have life more abundantly. You choose. Which Kingdom do you choose to live in? Good or evil?**

So in Summary:

- Who you are is "within you" and can never be changed, but, you choose your destiny.

- **God has great plans for you. Your destiny is chosen by God, but its fulfillment is determined by your choices. You decide and must make the right choices. Every choice and decision has consequences, successes and failures. Ponder your footsteps, get good godly council before making major decisions. Don't be a fool like I was in some of my bad choices and choke on the dust of regret later! Listen, we all make mistakes but there is FORGIVENESS and HOPE for your future if you make the right choices now and repent from your past. You have no need to tell**

your sins to some priest. That's simply "intelligence gathering" by a corrupt religious system started centuries ago. Go directly to God your Heavenly Father, through Christ.

- Your future has been predestined, but it's up to you if you arrive there. In other words, you could be anointed and called by God in music, but you sing for the devil. Your calling is "within you" but your influence is on the "Kingdom of darkness" rather than singing for "the Kingdom of light" and being the light in darkness. The result is frustration and never manifesting your full potential God called you to. The end result is disillusion, frustration, and misery.

- **It takes just as much effort and faith to believe you can succeed in God's calling as it does to fail under the dark influences of Satan's deceptions.**

- Depression is a symptom of not knowing your purpose. The secret key to success in your life is to find your gift "within you." This gift is attached to your purpose for being here on planet earth to solve a problem. As you help others and you are anchored "in Christ" and "His Kingdom" you drive out darkness and overcome depression through your purpose for living and helping others.

- **Your gifting(s) and purpose become your source of true leadership and "peace within," that passes all understanding. Education is not the key to success in life, it doesn't guarantee anything; it is your gift that is the key to your success.**

- You are here to make the world a better place. To have life in a world of chaos, confusion, fear, uncertainty, doubt, hopelessness, death, and destruction...controlled by Satan's Kingdom is very depressing...That's why we need Christ and His

Kingdom...not religion and all it's watered down, misdirected concepts and mis-conceptions of truth!

- **The war is between "the Kingdom of Darkness", and "the Kingdom of Light" within your soul. The one you choose is the winner of your soul of which you will spend eternity with. You get what you choose.**

  Your riches will be where your heart is. If your heart is to see souls saved and brought into the Kingdom of God...your heart efforts, finances, goals, and energies will lean into that Kingdom. Which Kingdom are all your energies focused on? This gives you a true reading of your heart. Be honest with yourself, be detailed. What do you want to change if anything? This is your eternal destiny.

Notes, Thoughts, Ideas

Observations, things I want to Change in my life...and new understandings.

Question #4

<u>What Is My Destiny</u>

Your future destiny has been determined by God, but its fulfillment is determined by you. God has given you a "FREE WILL". You are not a robot controlled by a Tyrant. (That's Satan's Kingdom of darkness) to rob, steal, kill and destroy your life. God loves you, Christ died for you. You choose your destiny, light or darkness, right or wrong, heaven or hell.

- We must give an answer to how the entire universe came into being and the "reason why" we are here on planet earth right now.

Here are a few facts

- **It took a miracle to set the stars in place with His fingertips, the heavens his throne, and the earth his footstool. When God said, "Let there be L-I-G-H-T! Light shot out at 186,000 miles per second and is still traveling at that speed. This is nothing to fool with.**

- Ephesians 3: 9 & 10 says: And to make all men see what is the fellowship of the mystery, which from the beginning of the world has been hid in God who created all things by Jesus Christ:
  10) To the intent that now unto the principalities and powers in heavenly places might be known by the church *(you and me if you're in His Kingdom)* the manifold wisdom of God.

- **Hebrews 11:3 states: By faith we understand that the worlds were set in order at God's command, so that the visible has its origins in the invisible. God's Kingdom is the oldest, most powerful Kingdom in the universe!**

Listen: Science has now proven there's over 100 Billion galaxies with over One Billion Trillion stars and God's word says, "He knows every star by name!" Now that's power! You scoffers better wake up before it's too late for you.

- We call this great Creator God. God is the "Almighty Creator" of creation and we "His children" are creative. There is only One True God. Satan is the god of deception. So, then, we did not evolve from polly wog soup, turn into tadpoles, come out of the soup, climb trees, turn into monkeys, evolve into mankind and here we are. That's the best clumsy, stupid explanation that a fallen man's corrupted, blinded minds can come up with. And this garbage is taught in our schools, colleges and universities! No wonder there's such confusion, despair, depression, violence, gun massacres, terrorism, and suicidal self-destruction. This is the outward manifestation of "the Kingdom of Darkness" within man's wicked, evil, corrupted heart from the first Adam's fall into self-centeredness, twisted deception, greed, violence, power, and corruption.

- **The "Kingdom of God" is where the will of the King is being done. The Father, the Almighty Creator has a Kingdom. When we surrender our life to Christ and Repent from our sins...he is the doorway back into the "Kingdom of God."**

- All religions are man's attempt to "find the Kingdom" and the "reason why" we are here on planet earth.

- The Kingdom of God within the first Adam was lost to Satan. Satan became the ruler of man and the "god of this world." Satan comes as an angel of light with great cunning deception. All his false religions sound good, very religious sounding, look good, stained glass windows, pipe organs, long black or white gowns, but rebellion, and pride, and corrupt filthiness are at the root of his deceptions resulting in heartache, tears, and the weeping and gnashing of teeth (blaming others) on the Judgement day. Satan is not the god of the earth. He is "the god of this world" which "rules over the earth." Satan is the trouble maker and terrorist creating hell on earth through man's rebellion toward God. God won't stop him right now but you can...through Christ in you! (more on this in the next journal).

- **When Jesus entered His ministry at age 30 Satan tempted Him. In Matthew 4:8-10 the devil takes Jesus into an exceedingly high mountain and shows him all the "Kingdoms of the world," and the glory of them;**

9) And Satan said to Jesus, "All these things will I give you if you will fall down and worship me. (This is the war within). Satan wants you to follow him. To sing his songs of rebellion, loneliness, sadness and death. Satan wants you to worship him and raise your hands to all these "worldly idolized" singers and entertainers.

10) Jesus said, "Get thee out of here Satan for it is written, you shall "worship the Lord your God" and "him only" shall you serve. Where do you think Satan got all the Kingdoms and how did he get them? He stole them from the first Adam through deception! The first Adam did not lose a religion. He lost the Kingdom rulership God gave him to rule and reign over the earth. Satan set up his Kingdom here on earth and made it a deceptive religious system. That's how and why we are in this mess right now. Soon it will be over when Christ sets up His Kingdom here on earth at the battle of Armageddon, when

Russia "The Bear of the North" and its allies try to destroy Israel.

- Jesus did not bring back a religion. He brought back "the Kingdom" that the first Adam lost. Jesus preached "the Kingdom." His biggest problem was not the sinner but the religious people. And it's still that way today. Religion is a big problem. Religion creates all kinds of wars. Satan is the god of religion. Jesus is the King of Gods Kingdom. Big difference!

- **Seek first the Kingdom of God and His righteousness (right standing with God) and all these things (you need) will be added unto you.**

- The Bible "God's word" is NOT a religious book!

- **The Bible calls itself a testament. A testament is a covenant. It's a contract. It's a constitutional contract which contains the constitutional rights of its citizens in a Kingdom ruled by a King. The problem is always religious minded people with a wrong concept.**

- The Bible is about a King, a Kingdom, and His Royal family who have chosen to be governed by Kingdom principles.

- **A Kingdom is not a religion. It's not governed by a president or a prime minister. It is a country, governed through a set of laws ruled by a King, over its citizens. Our King is Jesus Christ who loved us enough to die for us!**

- The Bible is all "Kingdom terminology" that when fully understood will transform your life and move you from religious darkness into Kingdom royalty and citizenship, not as a "member" of some "religious organization"...but a "citizen" of a "Kingdom".

- **The Bible is about a government that will ultimately dominate the planet (when Jesus returns and establishes Kingdom rulership on earth). His Kingdom has come (for those who believe), and is coming in the fullness when he comes back to Jerusalem to rule and reign.**

- A Kingdom then, is a country that reflects the will and the culture of the King. In this case it's a "heavenly Kingdom and a heavenly culture."

- **A Kingdom is a nation under a King's rule and its Royal citizens have no rights because the King provides all you have need of through his commonwealth and citizenship (Christ's church). The King owns everything. You are not your own. The money He blessed you with is not yours. It's His. He owns you if He is Lord of your life. He bought and paid for you with His blood. The body of Christ takes care of itself through the leadership of the King. Jesus is the "King of kings" you and I are kings in God's Kingdom. We are ambassadors in God's Heavenly Kingdom on earth. This is the "good news".**

- This is renewing your mind to "Kingdom of God" principles. This "good news" creates "inner transformation."

- **To be a citizen in the Royal family and receive your rightful inheritance in the "Kingdom of God" makes you an ambassador here in the earth representing the Kingdom of Heaven. Our prayer should be as Jesus prayed and preached. "Thy Kingdom come, Thy will be done on earth as it is in heaven."**

- You are then a problem solver earning a living through leadership in a problem solving business or ministry while managing God's resources like forestry, water, energy etc. NOT blowing the earth up like little rocket man!

- **Your destiny is ultimately heaven or hell based on your choice of the Kingdom you choose to live in now. There is no purgatory and a second chance later. There's no Reincarnation and coming back as a pig or a chicken or a rat like the Hindus and their six million gods believe. Listen; there's only one you. You are special. You have one chance right now. You better get it right. God loves you. I deeply care about your soul. But you Decide. What you choose...you get! Repent, choose Christ...and walk in His Holy righteousness!**

- Romans 12: 1 & 2 gives us guidance:
  I beseech you therefore brethren, by the mercies of God, that you present your bodies a living sacrifice, (No more drugs, alcohol cursing God, murder, adultery, terrorist thinking and self abuse) holy, acceptable unto God, which is your reasonable service.
  2) And be not conformed to this world! But be **TRANSFORMED** (inner transformation) by the renewing of your mind, (to the Word of God) that you may prove what is that good, and acceptable, and perfect will of God. God is a Holy God. Therefore walk in His Holiness.
  Romans 14:17 declares:
  The Kingdom of God is not meat and drink; (its not outward but inward) but righteousness, peace and joy in the Holy Ghost. If you want "peace within"...you must invite the "Prince of Peace" Jesus Christ to come and live in your heart. *This is the only way you will win the "war within!"*

In Summary

Revelation 19: 11-16

And I saw heaven opened, and behold a white horse; and he that sat upon him was called Faithful and True, and in righteousness he doth judge and make war. His eyes were as a flame of fire, and on his head were many crowns; and he had a name written, that no man knew, but he himself. And he was clothed with a vesture dipped in blood: and his name is called "**The Word of God**". And the armies which were in heaven followed him upon white horses, clothed in fine linen, white and clean. And out of his mouth goeth a sharp sword, that with it he should smite the nations: and he shall rule them with a rod of iron: and he treadeth the winepress of the fierceness and wrath of Almighty God. And he hath on his vesture and on his thigh a name written, **KING OF KINGS, and LORD OF LORDS.**

So, your destiny is...what you ultimately choose. Jesus is the King...of Kings (you are a king in His Royal Kingdom if you choose).

If you choose man-made religion (which is seeking to go to heaven) and think you're going to heaven because you're just a good person..."your soul is in grave danger of hell." Why? Because we will be in a "Heavenly Kingdom" ruling on earth! That's the difference between "Religion teaching heaven", and "Christ preaching The Kingdom!" Choose life. Your final destiny is your choice, and what you choose, you get.

Notes, Thoughts, Ideas

Observations, things I want to Change in my life...and new understandings.

Understanding "The Kingdom of God Within You"

Kingdom: 4469 Hebrew: Mannlakah means: Kingdom, dominion, reign, realm, royal rule, sovereignty.

932 Greek Basileia: Royal Dominion, belonging to, appointed, suitable for a king, Royal Priesthood, Royal dignity, A King, Monarch, to reign or have predominance.

Adam turned his dominion (given to him by God) over to Satan in the garden of Eden. Adam not only fell into self-centeredness and sin, but became a slave to fear and death, taking on the Luciferic nature. He lost his Kingdom rulership and was kicked out of the garden.

Isaiah 8: 6 & 7 declares: For unto us a child is given! (Jesus) and the government (there needs to be a country or Kingdom to have a government) shall be upon his shoulder: and his name shall be called Wonderful, Counselor, The Mighty God, The Everlasting Father, The Prince of Peace.

7) Of the increase of His government (In His Kingdom) and peace there shall be no end, upon the throne of David and upon "**HIS KINGDOM**", to order it and to establish it with judgement and with justice from henceforth even forever. The zeal of the Lord of hosts will perform this.

Zechariah 14:9: And the Lord shall be King over all the earth: in that day shall there be one Lord and His name one.

Note: The first Adam lost the Kingdom...not a religion. The second Adam (Jesus Christ) brought back and paid for the Kingdom (not a religion) lost by the first Adam. This Kingdom of God is our inheritance if we are "Born Again" citizens through Christ and have repented from our sins.

That's why we are to "seek first the Kingdom of God and His righteousness" (right standing with God) and "all these things you have need of will be added unto you"

Here are just a few of over 60 scriptures of the "Kingdom of God" that Jesus preached...yet we rarely ever hear them preached today! Why? Because this message of the "Kingdom of God" got lost through the dark ages of Catholicism that will be judged according to Revelation 17:5.

Note: Gospel: 2098 Euaggelion; means: The "good news" of the "Kingdom of God" and salvation through Christ. Jesus' message was most always about "the Kingdom" not of Himself.

In Matthew 3:1-2-3 John the Baptist introduced Christ to the world preaching **"Repent for the 'Kingdom of Heaven' is at hand"**, which was spoken of by the prophet Isaiah prophesied in Isaiah 8:6 & 7. Up until this time the law and the prophets in the old testament (covenant contract) was being preached. John the Baptist had one foot in the old testament and one foot in the **"NEW"** Covenant which was the gospel...the "good news" that "**The Kingdom of God**" was being brought back to a lost humanity!

- Luke 4:43 And Jesus said unto them, **"I must preach the Kingdom of God to other cities also: for that is why I was sent."** Jesus mostly preached "The Kingdom of God." He told His disciples to preach the "Kingdom of God." Matthew 10:28 Why is the "Kingdom of God" not preached today? The messages today are everything "but" the Kingdom of God! Are we hearing another gospel? The Kingdom of God is not even taught in Bible schools! Why?

- **Jesus went about teaching and preaching the "Kingdom of God" and healing all manner of sickness and disease. Matthew 4: 23 (Notice that** sickness and disease was healed as Jesus, and His disciples preached "The Kingdom of God"). Jesus was God manifested in the flesh! Shouldn't we be preaching the same message He preached? He commanded His disciples to preach it. Yet we never hear it preached today. We hear another gospel being preached. We are to preach the "good news" of the "Kingdom of God."

- Yours is the "Kingdom of Heaven". Matthew 5:3 (the believer)

- **Yours is the "Kingdom of Heaven". Matthew 5:10 (the believer)**

- There are those who shall be called "the least and the greater" in the Kingdom of Heaven. Matthew 5:19

- **You CAN NOT enter the "Kingdom of Heaven" accept through righteousness. Christ is our righteousness. (Right standing with the father) and not through religion like the scribes and Pharisees. Matthew 5:20**

- Jesus prayer was "Thy Kingdom come, Thy will be done on earth as it is in heaven." Matthew 6:10 God's will is to extend his Kingdom from heaven into the earth through his royal family. The first Adam lost The Kingdom. Jesus, the second Adam, bought the Kingdom back! Today we hear a gospel of everyone accepting Christ (which is right) but the emphasis is on "going to heaven." The message Christ preached was for "The Kingdom of Heaven to come to earth." All religions are preaching heaven bound and Christ is teaching and preaching that "He" was the "door-way" into the "Kingdom of God" to be set-up on earth. Two different gospels. Two different emphasis. I am choosing to preach the gospel Christ preached, which is "The Kingdom of

God" message, not the heaven the false religious system is preaching.

- **Matthew 6:13 states; For yours is the "Kingdom", and the power and the glory, forever. Amen. We will live in God's Kingdom forever so you better know and understand your destiny. And your purpose.**

- Jesus said seek "first" the Kingdom of God and his righteousness and all these things will be added unto you. Matthew 6:33 He didn't promote himself first. He was promoting His Kingdom first. He is the "doorway" into His Kingdom.

- **Not everyone will enter "the Kingdom of Heaven", but only the ones who "DO" the will of the Father who is in heaven. Matthew 7:21**

- **Galatians 5:19** Declares clearly: Now the works of the flesh (or our old sin nature) are manifested which are these, adultery, fornication, (incest and homosexuality) uncleanness, lustfulness (perverted filthiness).
  20) Idolatry (idol worship) witchcraft, hatred, variance (quarreling, contention, debate and strife) wrath (fierce indignation) strife, seditions, (dissension and division) heresies, (disunity).
  21) Envying, murders, drunkenness, reveling (carousal, rioting, terrorism) and such like: of which I tell you before and, have also told you in time past, that they which do such things **SHALL NOT INHERIT THE KINGDOM OF GOD**.
  Note: That's why Jesus preached **"REPENT"** for the Kingdom of God is at hand.

- **Note:** In some of these verses the "Kingdom of Heaven" more particularly signifies God's rule within us while here on earth. When we "The Born

Again Believers" die we go to paradise but we are coming back to earth with Christ to set up His Kingdom, and we will rule and reign for the 1000 year millennial reign. Then...the Great White Throne judgement and a new heavens and a new earth.

- **Jesus went preaching and teaching "the gospel" of "the Kingdom" and healing every sickness and disease. Matthew 9:35 Sickness and disease (disease or lack of ease) is in Satan's Kingdom of darkness. That's why Christ preached "The Kingdom of God" and drove out and destroyed sickness and disease. Light overcomes darkness. We are to overcome evil with good. Jesus went about doing good and healing all that were "oppressed of the Devil!" Oppression, insanity and depression are manifestations of the Kingdom of Darkness, Death and Destruction.**

- Jesus commanded His disciples **"TO DO"** exactly as he did. Preach the "Kingdom of Heaven" is at hand...heal the sick, cleanse the lepers, raise the dead and cast out devils. Matthew 10:7 & 8. This is the "Kingdom of Light" over the Kingdom of darkness within man's soul that Satan stole from the first Adam's fall. This is the gospel we must be preaching today! This is the only way **"TO WIN THE WAR WITHIN."**

- **We as Born-Again believers are to know, seek, learn and understand the "mysteries" of the "Kingdom of Heaven." Matthew 3:11**

- When you hear the gospel, the good news of the Kingdom, and understand it, Satan will try to steal the word, that "*word seed*," sown in your heart. Matthew 13:19.

I remember the day I got saved back in 1974. I was suicidal. I had been only seconds away from pulling the trigger. I heard the "good news" of the gospel. I surrendered my life to Christ. I repented and stopped gambling, stopped stealing with the cards, got delivered from heavy drugs and alcohol...instantly! I was so excited. I was raised Roman Catholic and had never heard the real gospel preached. It was all plastic religious form. I went home immediately and told my mom and dad what happened. I was so excited and transformed instantly. My dad got so angry (because he was Roman Catholic and was never taught to read the bible for himself), that he immediately kicked me out of the house! That was Satan trying to *"steal that word seed"* sown in my heart that day. Obviously it didn't work because my conversion was genuine. True believers will be persecuted. I was instantly persecuted by my family. Religious people will persecute you. They persecuted Jesus. But hold fast to Christ. Walk in "His Kingdom" for "Greater is He who is in you" than Satan which is the god of this world.

- **Study all of Matthew 13: 24-58. Jesus is teaching here on the "Kingdom of God" or the "Kingdom of Heaven." They are basically one and the same. Preaching The Kingdom of God opens the door to introduce Christ as "the doorway into" the Kingdom. Jesus rarely taught about Himself, the blood, the cross, the resurrection and so on. (That was all the necessary steps to pay the gruesome price to get the Kingdom back). He taught "The Kingdom". The Kingdom is so great there are many, many keys to enter into all the rooms in this Amazing, Great, Wonderful Kingdom. (more on the "keys to the Kingdom" Christ gave us in our next 30 day journal of your destiny "In Christ" in "His Kingdom"). There are simply too many keys to deal with in this introduction to the**

Kingdom of God and His Righteousness within you.

- Jesus said he has given us the keys of the Kingdom of Heaven to bind (to lock up) and to lose (to unlock) on earth as it is in heaven. Matthew 16:19

- **Many saw the Son of Man (Jesus) "coming in his Kingdom glory." Matthew 16:28 Jesus after his death, burial and resurrection returned and appeared to over 500 people over a 40 day period, and the birth of the church on the day of Pentecost introduced "the Kingdom of God" as our New Covenant Contract with Almighty God and Christ as our redeemer. (The new testament is a legal document and Kingdom contract between a King, a Kingdom and its citizens).**

- There is but one gospel. Jesus declared, "**THIS GOSPEL**" of "THE KINGDOM" will be proclaimed throughout the whole world as a testimony (it will be tested) to all nations and "**then**" **will the end come**. Matthew 24:14   If any **man** preach any other gospel (other than **THIS** Gospel)...let him be accursed. Wow! We better be preaching and teaching the "Kingdom of God" the message that Jesus preached...or...it's another gospel with a "wrong concept"...which leads into error and false religion!

- **The Kingdom of Heaven is likened unto ten virgins, five were walking in the anointing of the almighty power of the Holy Ghost and five weren't. Which are you. Anointed, seeking and walking in that anointing or just wandering around aimlessly hoping you are? (Or even worse...preaching the Kingdom of God...but living a lifestyle in the Kingdom of Satan!) Matthew 25:1-13. Study carefully and tremble!**

- Study Matthew 25: 14-46 Study this chapter. Read it fifty times and get a revelation on the seriousness yet excitement of the entire chapter and all the meanings of "The Kingdom of God" that Jesus preached and taught. He then told His disciples to preach the "Kingdom of God" in the Book of Acts after He appeared to over 500 people for a space of 40 days after His death, burial and resurrection. Why do we not hear the preaching of this message of the "Kingdom of God" today? There's not even a course in the bible schools. Yet this is the message of Christ. Seek first "The Kingdom of God!" He's not teaching on the blood, the cross, the resurrection or about Himself. He is teaching on "what the Kingdom of God" is like. He's teaching in parables. The true and deeper meanings are in the spiritual understanding of those seeking Truth. The cross, the shed blood and the resurrection were critical...they were the necessity and means and gruesome price Christ had to pay to..."buy the Kingdom back." Jesus' message was always the "good news" of the Kingdom, NOT Himself! Our message...must be the same message "of the Kingdom" to be preached around the world...then...will the end come!

- **When you walk in "understanding" of this glorious Kingdom message, you will come into a realization that the King is responsible in His Kingdom for His citizens. (And all these "things" you have need of) will be provided through His commonwealth...The same as if you were a citizen of the United States of America and it provides certain rights through its Constitution for its citizens.**

In Summary... It is your responsibility to "seek first" the Kingdom of God in all its manifestations, hungering and thirsting for God's presence and power both within yourself and within the body of Christ (the true believer) Matthew 6:33 and Mathew 5: 3, 5, 10.

In Matthew 11:12 Jesus tells us that Kingdom of God believers break away from sinful practices and turn to Christ, His Word and His righteous ways. This for some of us is a "vigorous war within!" My past was so ugly, so horrendous, I had so much to overcome. But I am overcoming by the blood of Jesus Christ, the word of my testimony and my determination to walk upright before God and man. Many times, I feel like such a failure. But I press on toward the work of my high calling "in Christ."

We must overcome evil with good. Flee temptation! Get out of the casinos if you have a gambling problem. Get out of the bars if you have a drinking problem! Seeking the Kingdom of God is a war!..."within." It requires earnest endeavors and a constant battle to overcome. It's a fight of faith. You must exercise a strong will to resist Satan and his Kingdom of dark temptations within, overcome temptation by a corrupt, perverted society...and win! That's how you **"WIN THE WAR WITHIN"**. You must press into the Kingdom of God, read his word, seek after his truths, get wisdom, get understanding and overcome. It's a heart war!

For good people it may be even harder. Why? Because you're such a good person you maybe can't even relate with a drunk, drug addicted, gambler or pervert. But make no mistake "we all have sinned and come short of the glory of God". Just one lie...makes you a liar. Where's your heart focused? Soul winning? Or just living in comfort and relying on being a good or nice person? Life is more than just having fun. Millions are going to hell. People are now fleeing the fires of California. Are you fleeing the fires of hell?

Notes, Thoughts, Ideas

Observations, things I want to Change in my life...and
new understandings.

What is a Kingdom?

First of all, a Kingdom is not a democracy, a republic nor a religion. It is 100% the opposite!

1. According to Webster's dictionary: A Kingdom is a Kings influence over a people and their domain. The King rules...not the people.

2. In a Kingdom, the King influences the people...not the people influencing the King.

3. A Kingdom is a sovereign rulership over a territory.

4. A Kingdom is the governing impact of a Kings will, intent, and purpose over a territory (in this case it is God's will and sovereignty of His Heavenly Kingdom over earth).

5. A Kingdom is a territory with a legal system and structure as "The Kingdom of God's" structure...NOT religion!

6. A Kingdom is a government led by a King impacting a territory (Earth). Like the United Kingdom of Britain ruling over Canada. Its rulership is an extension of its will over a territory. Turn off your religious mentality and look at and read God's word from His Kingdom point of view...not religion!

7. In a Kingdom, there is a constitution (a covenant contract with its citizens). The bible lays out clearly our inherent citizenship rights in the commonwealth of God's Kingdom here in the earth. (Not religion!)

8. A Kingdom has moral codes of conduct.

9. A Kingdom has shared values.

10. A Kingdom has a culture and a "body of laws" to protect its citizens from falling into misconception and error resulting in loss and destruction.

11. In a Kingdom its citizens reflect the culture and lifestyle of the King. Religion makes you a member of their church. In God's Kingdom when you are "born again" you become a citizen of His Kingdom. Big difference! A total different mindset. Remember: We are not to be conformed to this worlds way of thinking but be ye **TRANSFORMED BY THE RENEWING OF YOUR MIND TO THE WORD OF GOD!**

12. The "Kingdom of God" and all man-made religions will ultimately be..."must be"...separated from the Kingdom of darkness (Satan) and all his followers of man-made religions philosophies, theories, deceptions, rebellion to truth, propaganda and outright lies of the world.

God's Word is God's Will

2 Peter 1: 20-21

20) Knowing this first, that no prophecy of the scripture is of any private interpretation.

21) For the prophecy came not in old time by the will of man; but holy men of God spoke as they were moved by the Holy Ghost.

The author of this little journal believes that...

GOD'S WORD IS FINAL AUTHORITY!

Revelation 22: 18-21

For I testify unto every man that hears the words of the prophecy of this book, if any man (including popes, bishops, priests, preachers, Mormons, J.W.'s, or other religious cults) "shall add" unto these things, God shall add unto them the plagues that are written in this book.

19) And if any man shall "take away" from the words of the book of this prophecy, God shall take away his part out of

the book of life, and out of the holy city, and from the things which are written in this book.

20) He which testifies these things (Jesus Christ) says, "Surely I come quickly:" Amen. Even so come Lord Jesus.

21) The grace of our Lord Jesus Christ be with you all. Amen.

Dear reader; If you are a religious person, deceived in some man-made religious system, repent, come out of it...and enter into "The Kingdom of God," through Christ. You say, "but I have a different faith". Well...the word "faith" means "reliance upon Jesus". So if you believe differently that's fine. But it's not faith. It's a belief. Faith is a spiritual substance not a religious belief.

Seek first "The Kingdom of God" and his "righteousness" (right standing with God) and all these things (God knows your needs) will be added unto you.

Become a Kingdom citizen and receive your inheritance of your rightful Kingdom established before the foundation of the earth.

The first Adam, through deception by Satan and rebellion against God, lost the Kingdom to Satan, which is now the god of this world, which has blinded the minds of those who don't believe.

Jesus the only begotten Son of God, the Lamb of God, which has taken away the sins of the world has paid the price in full for you to be free from the sins and addictions that control your life. Jesus is your righteousness and the door...into His Kingdom. "The Kingdom" is our destination and there's only one door. Jesus is not our final destination. The Kingdom is. Jesus paid a dear price to get you there. He's the door. There's no other way in.

This Truth sets you FREE and gives you power to overcome.

You are only FREE when you live in God's Kingdom NOT man's religion (more on this in the next journal).

John 3: 16, 17 & 36

16) For God so loved the world, that He gave His only begotten Son, that whoever believes in Him should not perish, but have everlasting life.

17) For God sent not his Son into the world to condemn the world; but that the world through Him might be saved.

36) He that believes in the Son (not religion) has everlasting life; and he that does not believe in the Son shall not see life; but the wrath of God abides on him.

Dear reader; God loves you, Jesus died for you to deliver you from the Kingdom of darkness and make you a part of a Royal Family in a Royal Kingdom.

The war for your soul is the Kingdom of light and the Kingdom of darkness...warring within you! That's the war within and it's being played out on the battleground of your mind.

Buddha, Mohammad, Joseph Smith of the Mormons, the pope, or the virgin Mary never died for you and shed their blood for their followers. Your sin must be dealt with. Meditation of your mind, going to church every Sunday, being a good person, means nothing in God's Kingdom! If it did...Christ would not have had to go to the cross!

The fear of the Lord is the "beginning" of wisdom. Walking in the religious traditions of man or the deception of professors, psychologists, psychiatrists and other such nonsense will result in a mis-conception of the truth of "The Kingdom of God" and his righteousness and result in hell on the **GREAT WHITE THRONE JUDGEMENT DAY.**

Colossians 2:8 states clearly: Beware lest any man spoil you through philosophy and vain deceit, after the tradition of men, after the outward worldly institutions of this world's greed, and not after Christ.

Make no mistake, there is but one mediator between God and man...the man Christ Jesus.

God doesn't care about our opinion, deceptive thoughts and intents or religious beliefs. There are many wolves in sheep's clothing, liars, anti Christs and deceivers saying, "they are the Christs" or their religious organization is the way.

They say, "Just become a member of our church, pay your tithes, give them your money, be religious, be a good person, call yourself a Christian, and show up on Sunday." What garbage and an abomination.

If they don't preach "The Kingdom of God" and the full gospel, like Jesus preached...get out of their religious system for it's about to be judged. Find a good local church that preaches and teaches the full gospel of the Kingdom and teaches Christ like Paul did.

Acts 28:26-31 Paul preached exactly what Jesus preached. He preached the "Kingdom of God" and teaching those things which concern the Lord Jesus Christ, with all confidence, no man forbidding him.

Paul preached the "Kingdom of God" and taught Christ to those who believed.

Listen; the "Kingdom of God" is the good news that we preach that we can be made whole again and get our inheritance of the Kingdom of God back. Jesus, the cross, the blood, and the resurrection were all "the means" of getting the Kingdom and our inheritance back. That was predestined from the beginning of the world.

Jesus is not our destination. The "Kingdom of God" is our final destination. Jesus is the "door" and "the way" into His Kingdom of which "He is the King"...of kings (which we are) Kings!

Have you chosen to accept Christ as your personal savior and Lord? Is your name written down in the Lamb's book of Life? What are you struggling with?

_____

_____

_____

_____

_____

_____

If you were to die today...are you sure you will be with God throughout eternity through Christ?

_____

_____

Based on what?

_____

_____

If you are not sure and you want to be sure simply email me at 100safeandsecure@gmail.com and someone will be in contact with you if I am too swamped to contact you personally.

Notes, Thoughts, Ideas

Observations, things I want to Change in my life...and new understandings.

Understanding Our Loving Heavenly Father as Royal Children In His Kingdom

1. God is intimate, loving and involved with his Royal family. Read Psalms 139: 1-18

2. **God our Heavenly Father is kind and compassionate. Read Psalms 103: 8-14**

3. God our Heavenly Father is filled with kindness and love. Read Zephaniah 3:17 and Romans 15:7

4. **God our Heavenly Father is warm and affectionate. Read Isaiah 40:11 and Hosea 11:3,4**

5. God our Heavenly Father is always with you and eager to spend time with you if you seek him. Read Jeremiah 31:20, Ezekiel 34:11-16 and Hebrews 13:5

6. **God our Heavenly Father is patient, slow to anger, loving, gentle, and protective of you "In Christ". Read Exodus 34:6, 2 Peter 3:9, Psalms 103:8, Psalms 18:2, Isaiah 42:3 and Jeremiah 31:3**

7. God our heavenly father is tender hearted and forgiving; His loving heart and arms are always open to you. Read Psalms 130:1-4 and Luke 15:17-24

Now...Go and "sin no more" but walk in His Loving Kindness and share the "good news" of His Kingdom.

Notes, Thoughts, Ideas

Observations, things I want to Change in my life...and
new understandings.

The Kingdom of God Brings Hope to The Hopeless!

Christ in Me the hope of glory! Colossian 1:27

We all need hope. When we repent from our sins, stop rebelling against God, turn from our man-made religion and get "Born Again" into the Kingdom of God...you are complete "in Christ."

Here are a few facts:

When you **"REPENT FROM YOUR SINS AND RELIGIOUS FORMS"** and accept Christ, the "Word of God" says...

- You are forgiven of your sins and washed in the shed blood of Christ. Ephesians 1:7

- **You are a new creature or new creation in Christ. 2 Corinthians 5:17**

- You are delivered from the darkness of Satan's Kingdom and translated into God's Kingdom. Colossians 1:13

- **You are redeemed from the curse of the law. Galatians 3:13**

- You are accepted in Christ. Ephesians 1:6

- **You are crucified with Christ. Galatians 2:20**

- You are raised up with Christ and seated in heavenly places in His Kingdom. Colossians 2:12

- **You are called of God. 2 Timothy 1:9**

- You are brought near by the blood of Christ. Ephesians 2:13

- **You are more than a conqueror. Romans 8:37**

- You are an ambassador for Christ and His Kingdom. 2 Corinthians 5:30

- **You are born of God and the evil one does not touch you. 1 John 5:18**

- You are a joint heir with Jesus and inherit the Kingdom. Romans 8:17

- **You are reconciled to God. 2 Corinthians 5:18**

- You are a fellow citizen with the saints of the household of the Kingdom of God. Ephesians 2:19

- **You are sealed with the promise of the Holy Spirit. Ephesians 1:13**

- You are complete in Christ. Colossians 2:10

- **You are free from condemnation. Romans 8:1**

- You are the righteousness of God through Jesus Christ. 2 Corinthians 5:21

- **You are now a disciple of Christ because you have love for others. John 13:34-35**

- You are a partaker of His divine nature in the Kingdom of God. 2 Peter 1:4

- **You are now God's workmanship. Ephesians 2:10**

- You are now being changed into His image. Philippians 1:6

- **You are now one with Christ in His Kingdom. John 17:21-23**
- You have all your needs met according to His glorious riches in Christ Jesus. Philippians 4:19

- **You have everlasting life. John 6:47**

- You have a guaranteed inheritance of the Kingdom. Ephesians 1:14

- **You have abundant life. John 10:10**

- You have overcome the world. 1 John 5:4

- **You have the peace of God which passes all understanding. Philippians 4:7**

- You have access to the Father by one spirit. Ephesians 2:18

- **Greater is He who is in you than Satan who is in the world. 1 John 4:4**

- You are now a saint "in Christ". Ephesians 1:1

Read these daily. Renew your mind. *Come out of man-made religions. Repent and stop sinning.* Walk in Christ. Walk and live in the "Kingdom of God". Seek first the "Kingdom of God" and His "Righteousness" and all things you need will be added to you. The Kingdom of God, in Christ, is "within you!"

Listen dear reader. There are only two Kingdoms. You've got to serve somebody. "**Jesus Christ** in the Kingdom of God" or "Satan in the Kingdom of darkness and the "anti-

Christ" in man-made religions." Satan is the god of this worlds false religious systems.

A sharp line is drawn between good and evil, "God" is the root word of "good". "Evil" is the root word of D-evil. A sharp line is drawn between darkness and light, life and death, children of God and children of Satan's false religions, the righteous and the wicked, wheat and tares (false wheat) saved and lost, not condemned and the condemned because of prideful rebellion, heaven and hell, selfishness and love. These are sharp contrasts between the "Kingdom of God" and the "Kingdom of Satan," with no 50 shades of grey compromises! You are either "IN Christ" or you are "IN sin and anti-Christ" and Satan's religious system according to Revelations 17:1-18.

You now have a clear choice. The Kingdom of God through Christ...or remain...in the deception of the Kingdom of Satan and man-made religions. You choose for eternity...because both will inevitably be...**"separated for eternity."** Who you choose as your King is where you will spend eternity. That's how you get to choose your destiny. Choose life! Choose Christ and live in "His Kingdom."

Who do you choose?

_____

_____

_____

Why?

_____

_____

_____

_____

For God so loved the world,
that he gave his only begotten Son,
that whosoever believeth in him should
not perish, but have everlasting life. For God sent
not his Son into the world to condemn the world;
but that the world through him might be saved.
John 3:16 - 17

Notes, Thoughts, Ideas

Observations, things I want to Change in my life...and
new understandings.

Who Do I Choose to Serve... God or Satan?

You've got to serve somebody. God through Christ and His Kingdom...or...Satan through false religions and his Kingdom of darkness. What is your belief system? Don't go into denial. This is serious. This is your life. It's between you and your Creator. Open your heart to Him.

My Belief is...	What Does God's Word Say?

What is your eternal destiny now based on your belief system compared to God's word?

Why all Man-made Religions are tied into the synagogue of Satan and his Kingdom of darkness!

Ecclesiastes 9:3 declares:

"Madness was in their hearts while they lived." The word **madness** according to Webster's means mental illness, folly, foolishness, lunacy, craziness, turmoil, disorder, mayhem, chaos "insanity." So insanity and this full description of mental illness is in the heart of humanity. God judged it with "the flood" in the old testament. Violence is an outward manifestation of madness and insanity within the heart of the individual. That's why man reaches upward to an unknown God through their blinded minds because insanity is a mental disorder (dis-order out of order), leading to depression and suicidal self-destruction. That's why we hear of a murder, or mass murder, then the shooter takes their own life, like the Las Vegas massacre. Obviously madness or insanity ruled in his life! Insanity kills people...not guns, knives or bombs. Only insane people (even millionaires) pull the trigger! I know, I almost did!

This "madness" or "insanity" is also known as "sin" within the heart of man. When you find your purpose for living in the "Kingdom of God" through Christ, you are translated from the Kingdom of fear, uncertainty, doubt, anger, resentment, retaliation, lying, cheating, murder, deception, rebellion, pride, greed, arrogance, bitterness, sexual perversion, *and "you receive a spirit of love, power and a sound mind."* 2 Timothy 1:7 A sound mind means **Sanity!** You **"get your sanity back"** that was lost when the first Adam lost the Kingdom. *Sanity* and *righteousness* is a part of "The Kingdom of God" within you when you receive God's spirit of eternal life through Christ.

Listen dear reader: There are only two Kingdoms and two races of people. The Kingdom of darkness rules in the heart of the *"fallen race"* of the first Adam who turned his Kingdom over to Satan through rebellion against God

73

and...the Kingdom of Light rules in the heart of the *"resurrected race"* of the second Adam (Jesus Christ) who bought back the "Kingdom of God" the first Adam lost. The first Adam didn't lose a religion. He lost the Kingdom! Now it all depends on your choice "which Kingdom you choose to live in" that determines your eternal destiny. You're responsible for your life and your choices...not the government!

If you know someone in depression through a mental illness...they need their sanity back! Only Christ and living in His Kingdom will keep people **"sane"** in the brutal days ahead. Mental stability comes through sanity, given through eternal life in Christ.

Here are a few facts:

- Sin is a defilement that is at the root of insanity and violence within the heart of humanity and must be cleansed away. (That's why Jesus preached "Repent", for the "Kingdom of God" is at hand). "Repent" means to change your thinking and turn away from evil. That's the only way you will *"Win The War Within!"* Overcome evil with good. Overcome insanity within by surrender to Christ and repentance. This is a very real war between the two races for your soul...and...false religions are a distraction from the reality of your eternal destiny. This is a real life and death war you're in right now! That's why your choices are so critical!

- **Sin (mental illness, madness and insanity) is a heavy burden and must be lifted through forgiveness. (Forgiveness is the only way to unload the heavy burden of guilt, anger, resentment, retaliation, and bitterness (through madness or insanity of the unsaved) that eats**

74

away at your soul and often turns into cancer and manifests itself in your physical body). Thank God for forgiveness and divine healing through Jesus Christ and His shed blood on the cross at Calvary!

- Sin is a mighty debt which must be paid for in full by a redeemer. *(Jesus was the Lamb of God that paid the price in full on the cross).* No man can pay this price. You can be a multi-Billionaire, gain the whole world and spend eternity in hell with Satan's bunch of rebellious spirits against God!

- **"Sin" is a mountain between man and the "Kingdom of God" and must be removed. (Jesus removed it).**

- The first step toward the "Kingdom of Heaven" is to see clearly we are in the clutches of the Kingdom of Satan, mental illness, insanity, wrong concepts and our minds have been blinded to Truth and Spiritual realities. You may say, "I don't worship Satan, I just worship God in my own way." That's your problem! God made "the way"...and...Jesus is that way! Otherwise you're Anti-Christ. There is no other way because sin runs deep in the blood, soul and heart of man. Jesus' blood was "Royal Blood" with no sin taint because "God" was his Father. And...the blood in a child comes only from the father. The mother's blood is not in a child's veins. A child has their mothers genes...but not her blood. The life of the flesh is in "the blood". That's why the blood of Jesus cleanses us from all unrighteousness because his pure Royal Blood was from His Heavenly Father with no sin taint! (Read the book..."Chemistry of the Blood" by Dr. M.R. Dehaan)

1 Timothy 2:5-6 states clearly "There is One God and one mediator between God and men, the man Christ Jesus: 6) who gave himself a ransom for all.

Not all the popes that people call "Holy Father", not Mohamad, not Buddha, not Joseph Smith, not Harry Chrishna, Not Hinduism and its six million gods, images and statues nor any other religion of the world including Roman Catholicism and all its break away harlot daughters are the answer! Only Christ and His Kingdom! If there was "any other way" then Christ died in vane and you are slapping God in the face by saying differently! There are only two Kingdoms and two races of people. Pick one. The Kingdom of insanity. Or the Kingdom of sanity and a sound mind. You can't live in both and stay in your sanity.

John 3: 16 & 17 declares; For God so loved the world, that he gave his only begotten Son, that whosoever believeth in him should not perish, but have everlasting life.

17) For God sent not His Son into the World to condemn the world; but that the world through Him might be saved.

Listen: Jesus said in John 14:6, I am **THE WAY, THE TRUTH** and **THE LIFE** and no man comes to the father but by me.

John 10: 7-10 Jesus declared: "I am the door of the sheep."

8) All that ever came before me are thieves and robbers: but the sheep did not hear them.

9) **I AM THE DOOR**; by me if any man enter in, he shall be saved and shall go in and out (of His Kingdom) and find pasture.

10) The thief comes to rob, steal, kill and destroy: I am come that they might have life, and that they might have it more abundantly.

Jesus never preached that He was the Kingdom. He preached that He was **THE WAY, THE TRUTH** and **THE LIFE.** And...that He was the "door-way" into the Kingdom where there's abundance of life in God's Kingdom where He is the King and we are Royal family in His Kingdom.

It's a lie and deception by Satan and his deceivers that say there are many ways to God. Man's religions are deceptions of false hope to keep your eyes off Christ and keep you in bondage to addictions and loss of control over your life. Being "Born Again" into the Kingdom of God gives you love, joy, peace and a sound, sane, mental understanding. The war is on the battle field of your mind. It's a mental war!

Colossians 1:14 says "In Him" we have redemption through His blood, even the forgiveness of sins.

Sin must be dealt with upfront before anyone can enter back into the "Kingdom of God" and get back their sanity! Jesus Christ is the "doorway" into The Kingdom of God.

The Kingdom of God therefore is "not a religion" but "a country" ruled by a King. Jesus Christ is the King...of Kings. We are the royal family of kings ruling, reigning and driving the Kingdom of darkness out of those lost souls seeking the meaning of life or living in depression and insanity and contemplating suicide. *"Jesus" is the only way you will "WIN THE WAR WITHIN!"* Accept Christ now and get back your sanity! Repent from your sins. Walk in righteousness and true holiness.

Welcome into the "Kingdom of God." The Kingdom of God is your destination. Jesus is that "doorway" into the Kingdom of eternal life.

When Christ returns at the battle of Armageddon to set up His Kingdom on Earth for the thousand-year millennial reign...we will be ruling with Him. Praise God! We are coming back with Him. This is the message we must share with the lost. It's the "good news" of the Kingdom. People don't want to hear about Jesus. They don't want to hear about blood, spikes and the cross. They want hope. They want to know "why" they're here. They want to know how this "Kingdom of God" works. They want to know how they got here, what's their purpose here, how they can feed their family, get healing for their body. How they can overcome suicidal thoughts and other insane addictions. How to overcome depression with the false sorcery system of pharmaceutical drugs and all their weird deadly side effects! Then, you share and teach Christ! When you go fishing you don't say "hook" to the fish. You say "here's the worm" and they're attracted because they're hungry! Billions of people are hungry today to hear the "good news" of the Kingdom and God's love for them as hope. Jesus said, "follow me and I will make you fishers of men." What was His message? The Kingdom! He taught in parables of what the "Kingdom of God" was like. Read the whole book of Matthew and notice the teachings of Jesus on the Kingdom.

He said "Seek first...The Kingdom...then...the righteousness (which is Christ!) and how to live a holy life walking in righteousness.

Get your message right and your family and friends will flock into the Kingdom because they can rule over the nations with Christ as He sets up "His Kingdom" on earth! This is the "good news"...and "the Gospel" of the Kingdom of God that Jesus and his disciples preached.

I teach a full 3 hour "Soul Winning" session on the "key questions" to ask to open "the door" to "the Kingdom message" that attracts the lost and then how to Segway over to sharing Christ...as all the disciples did. If you are a sheperd of a little flock...or...have bible studies and would like to "Win souls to Christ" contact me at 100safeandsecure@gmail.com.

Notes, Thoughts, Ideas

Observations, things I want to Change in my life...and
new understandings.

The Amazing Wonders and Internal Power of Purpose

""The greatest tragedy in life is not death, but a life without purpose which ultimately leads to emptiness, loneliness, lack, limitation, suicidal thoughts and often times...self-destruction and premature death!"

- The poorest person in the world is a person without a dream, a purpose and a vision for their eternal destiny to help others.

- **Your purpose can be fulfilled only during the allotted time you have been given while here on planet earth, to accomplish it.**

- Purpose is when you know and understand what you were born to accomplish while here on planet earth.

- **When you have hope for your future because of knowing your purpose you have true riches.**

- Hard work and diligence are essential to success, but they require an internal motivation. That internal motivation is purpose and vision.

- **When your purpose is not known "within you", abuse is inevitable because others will try to manipulate and control you.**

- If you are creative, your Great Creator has hidden "within you"...your special gifting's, your purpose and your vision for your future, your journey and your destiny. Beware! Don't use your gifts and talents for Satan's Kingdom through rebellion against God!

- **Your purpose is more powerful than your plans.**

- You are here for a reason. You are valuable!

- **You are here to make the world a better place.**

- You are here to solve a problem with a solution.

- **You were born to win, but conditioned to lose! Teachers, parents or professors may say you're stupid, or, you'll never make it, or, you'll never get financing. How do they know what God has put in your heart as a gifting or talent?**

- Every human being (including you) was created with a "creative imagination" and "purpose" to influence your world surroundings.

- **This influence is to impact your environment in a positive manner through Christ and His wisdom.**

- Suicidal thoughts come from depression and depression comes from not understanding your purpose for being here. Drugs are **NOT** the solution. Knowing your purpose is. That's why everyone needs this little journal to help them on their journey and avoid depression, darkness, destruction and hell! Buy a few of these little journals and give them to friends and family as a "gift". That's using your brain and resources and helping others who are troubled and seeking for answers. Invest in souls, not stocks and bonds that will soon vanish! Souls are eternal!

- **Your purpose is the only thing that is right for you. It is intrinsically tied to your thoughts, imaginations, intentions and plans "within your spirit".**

- Your future is "within you". You possess your future now. Don't look outward. Look inward.

- **Your "future" is more "important" than your past.**

Your "future" is more "powerful" than your past.
Your "future" is more "valuable" than your past.

- We are here on planet earth for more than just a job working for someone 40 hours a week for 40 years, then retire and die! We are here on assignment. Everyone has a specific purpose for "being". **What's yours? What do you feel your calling, gifting(s) and talents are?**

_____

_____

_____

_____

_____

What Are My Gifts and Talents I enjoy doing?

Eg. I love music, singing, playing an instrument, writing music,

Or

I am a leader...or...a good manager.

Or, I am going to write a book to help others.

Or I have a good business idea.

Write out in detail.

_____

_____

_____

How Can Your Gifts and Talents make the World a Better Place to Live, or, How Will They Help Another Person?

What is a Problem Out in the World I Can Help to Solve?

What is the Root Cause of This Problem?

_____
_____
_____
_____
_____

What is the Main Benefit of Solving This Problem?

_____
_____
_____
_____
_____

What Kind of Problems Could I Solve With My Talents and Gifts That I Feel Compelled Inwardly Would Help or Encourage Others?

_____
_____
_____
_____
_____

What Must I do to Improve the Talent, Gift or Skill I Love To Do That I Could Turn Into a Business that People Would Pay Me Money to Solve This Problem?

Eg. Carpentry or a trade in housing (This is practical). Or...computer web-site design. Good homemaker, organizer, lawncare, house care, serving food, chef, etc. Whatever you enjoy...do it as unto the Lord.

It might be volunteer work at a Salvation Army, cooking or serving. Or...it might be a volunteer at a pet shelter...whatever you feel within your heart...is a part of your talent or purpose...Do it as unto the Lord while being a light and sharing "the good news of the Kingdom of God" within your community. You...are the light in your community. Share the good news of the Kingdom with others. Don't let them go to Hell if you can help it. If you war in your heart against fear of rejection...this is a war you must win within!

Notes, Thoughts, Ideas

Observations, things I want to Change in my life...and
new understandings.

The Power and Purpose of Vision

Where there is no vision the people perish and become lawless, unbridled, unruly, lawbreakers! Proverbs 29:18

Here are a few facts:

- Purpose is what you were born to do...vision gives your purpose clarity. Vision is critical or you fall apart.

- **Visionary leaders ask the question "what kind of history do I dream of making that will make the world a better place?" What will my friends and family say about me at my graveside? This is your vision to focus on for your future.**

- Vision is unlimited "potential" for your future.

- **Vision is not sight. Vision is seeing your inner future before it comes to pass. Walt Disney passed away before Disney World was completed. One of the contractors said to Walt's brother "It's sure too bad Walt isn't here to see this project now completed." Walt's brother responded "Walt saw it completed long before he ever started it!"**

- Vision empowers you from "within" and makes you believe in a better world ahead.

- **Vision chooses your future, your friends, your use of time, your priorities, your use of energy, which Kingdom you invest your money, your attitude in life, your life plan, and dictates your values. Without a vision, and purpose you become**

**depressed and die inside. Vision sees your future.
This is living in the "Kingdom of God" within
you.**

- Sight is the ability to see things as they are but
vision is the inner capacity to see things as they
could be.

- **If your vision is real...you will definitely have
challenges to prove it. Nelson Mandela went to
prison for his vision. Martin Luther King was
murdered for his dream and vision. Why?
Because it's a challenge to the "Kingdom of
Darkness" to stop, rob, steal, kill, divert and
destroy your life purpose and your vision to
completion! This is all out spiritual warfare!
(More on your spiritual armor in journal III).**

- Your vision of your future should be simple, clear
and empowering for your future and those around
you.

Listen dear reader; if you feel broken beyond repair, if
you have felt betrayed or you have made the worst
mistake of your life and there seems like there's no
hope...hold on...it's not the end. It's not finished yet.
You may see unworthiness, damaged goods within your
life...but God sees inner healing, hope, and a future for
you, you are not too far gone. You must envision
yourself as a winner...an overcomer. Religion sees
disaster. God sees eternal life. Repent, get up, keep
going. This is the power of vision! Without it you will
die! Choose life!

In Summary:

An entire forest is "within" the seed the same as your entire future is "within" you!

You are special. You are one-of-a-kind. You are the only one in God's creation with your set of natural abilities, gifts, talents, ideas and spiritual abilities.

You are unique. Be yourself, not someone else. No one on planet earth will ever look, talk, walk, perceive, think and be exactly like you. That's why you're so special. Make yourself valuable through personal self-discovery of your purpose for being here at this time to help others solve a problem and people will pay you for your help. This is living as a Kingdom citizen in the "Kingdom of God" and all these things will be added unto you.

God created you, and called you to a special calling no one else can do. That's your purpose. Your vision is the electrifying power and inner clarity of Almighty God "within you" to fulfill your calling in the allotted time given to you.

Notes, Thoughts, Ideas

Observations, things I want to Change in my life...and new understandings.

Time, Change and The Power of Planning.

The secret to life is managing time and change through planning and journaling your plans. Everyone has 24 hours in a day... what's your plan?

Here are a few facts:

- Life is simply changes through time. We are all allotted a certain amount of time but your life, or my life, can be called upon tonight! When you pass on to the other side you don't take a U-Haul full of your junk you gathered up here on earth with you. You only take what you have invested into the Kingdom of God with you. That's souls. Are you ready? Where would you spend eternity if you died tonight? We never know when our time is up!

- **A plan tells you what you want and what you don't want and which Kingdom you want to invest in.**

- Planning is applying your purpose and your vision in time. (We only have so much time...don't squander it away!)

- **Planning is documenting a pre-conceived determination based on your gifting's, talents, purpose and vision to time.**

- Write your ideas, thoughts and plans down on paper.

- **Planning is taking control of your future.**

- Planning determines your destination and charts your course according to your purpose and vision.

- **A good plan doesn't just show you where to go but it shows you how to get there.**

- Your purpose is your destination, your plan is how you get there. Jesus is not our final destination. The Kingdom of God and ruling and reigning with Christ is our final destination.

- **When you meet an obstruction, don't turn back...keep going. Detours happen in life, just make a plan B. It's dangerous to live in the land of limbo just wondering through life hoping and praying.**

- Without planning, your future could be fatal because there's no action...and...faith without works is dead.

- **You can plan your way out of depression by finding your purpose. You can plan your way to success if you follow your purpose.**

- People who aggressively pursue their purpose with a plan will attract the resources necessary to fulfill it.

- **Your dreams and purpose may be real "within you" but your plans written out on paper give them life!**

- Proverbs 20:18 states "to make plans by seeking wise advice." God puts the plan in your mind and heart as part of your spiritual journey and eternal destiny. You know what it is! But you must put your plans on paper and work out your purpose with His guidance through wisdom and understanding.

- **The best way to invent and create your future for success is to plan it.**

- You can't plow a field by turning it over in your mind...it takes action! You must be a doer of the Word of God!

- **Turn your thoughts, ideas, purpose and vision into a design with a "plan of attack".**

- If you fail to plan, you plan to fail.

- **Life is power "within you" asking you where you want to go. Give God your plan because He gave you your talents and gifting's and the freedom to choose your destiny. He will help, lead and guide you through.**

- If you have no plan, you have no destiny and you can fall into deception and depression. God works with doers who have a plan...he then guides you through. Don't give up, winners never quit and quitters never win. But the secret is to be motivated inwardly by God's calling on your life!

In Summary:

Ephesians 3:20 declares; My God is able to do exceedingly and abundantly above all you can ask, think or imagine...and planning is the greatest act of faith you can exercise to be successful in fulfilling your purpose, vision, mission and calling for solving a problem while here on planet earth...and....getting paid for it because a workman is worthy of his hire. If you don't work, you don't eat.

What's your plan? Where do you want to go?

_____

_____

_____

How do you plan to get there?

_____

_____

_____

In business, investors always want to see a "detailed business plan" or you can't get financing. What's you plan if the economy collapsed?

_____

_____

_____

What's your plan for light, heat, food and water if the power were knocked out for 3 months and it's 20 below zero in the middle of winter?

_____

_____

_____

This is planning.

Your Freedom to Choose

If you continue to think like you've always thought you'll continue to get what you've always got.

If you have problems surrounding you maybe you're not clear on your calling, your mission or your message.

Whatever is going on in your life today is based on your belief system and thought patterns. Everything that's confronting you now is an echo of yesterday's thoughts and actions.

This is why we must look closely at our life.

What you think about, you speak about, and what you speak about you bring about, for as a man **"thinks in his heart so is he"**.

To change your destiny you must change your thinking. That's why God's word says, "Be not conformed to this world but be **TRANSFORMED** by the **Renewing of your mind to the Word of God.**

This little journal is not about information but **"INNER TRANSFORMATION"**.

It's about your final **outcome. Your eternal Destiny.** What do you choose? Be detailed.

Combining Your Talent, Purpose, Vision, and Mission Together

For example, my talent or passion is writing and helping others "*struggling within*". My talent is helping them through God's love. This has taken me years to work on but I love it. My God given purpose then is to reach out and see souls saved through my writings. My vision then is to fulfill my purpose and "win the lost at any cost!" This then becomes my mission statement.

To be detailed I could then "*en-vision*" giving one of these journals to every inmate in prison. I can also see this journal as a *"Bible study"* in home meetings. I can also see this little journal as a *"soul winning course"*. So then, this becomes my mission. I can now plan out in detail (on my planning sheet) how to go about fulfilling this mission. Now...how do you see yourself moving forward with your talent, your purpose, your vision, and your mission? Be detailed as possible. Allow it to grow over time. God will lead and guide you by his Holy Spirit. Just write it out from your heart.

Summary Of Steps of How to Win the War Within

This is not about political correctness but spiritual correctness.

Matthew 7:13 & 14 declares: Enter ye in at the strait gate: for wide is the gate, and broad is the way, that leads to destruction, and many there be which go in thereat: Because strait is the gate, and narrow is the way, which leads unto life, and few there be that find it.

"The fact that there's a broad highway to hell and only a stairway to heaven says a lot about the anticipated traffic!"

A fiery hell is very real. I don't see people running into the fires of California right now. Common sense says "flee the fires"! Only an insane person would choose to go to hell and spend eternity there. Do you have friends headed there? Get this little journal to them today. They may not be here tomorrow and their blood will be on your hands if you could...but didn't!

Here are five Key Steps to Win the War Within:

Step #1

Repent for the Kingdom of God is at hand. Matthew 4:17

- *Repent means*: feel or express sincere regret or remorse about ones wrong doing or sin.
- **To turn from sin and dedicate oneself to the amendment of ones life.**
- To change one's mind and go in the right direction.

I remember the day I surrendered my life to Jesus Christ and got "Born Again" into His Kingdom by His spirit and got cleansed by His blood.

A great flood of guilt of the past, worry about the future and anger for today was lifted off my shoulders. Darkness...like a 500 pound gorilla left me and I was FREE! I repented of my sin and that day **"I WON THE WAR WITHIN!"**

Jesus became my Lord...not Satan! I came out of Satan's Kingdom of darkness and was instantly translated into the Kingdom of light. Jesus became my Lord. He bought my life with His blood.

Step #2 – Surrender to Christ

I repented that day. That was over 40 years ago now. I never went back to my evil wicked ways of stealing money with a deck of cards. I had so much to overcome but God delivered me from the big ones right off the start! Why? Because I was sincere and God knew my heart. As we grow as children in His spiritual Kingdom, God peels off the ugliness like an onion. He then rebuilds us into His children.

I threw the cards in the garbage. I have never picked them up since in over 40 years! I made millions of dollars with the cards. But...I started a new life that day. God dealt with my heart and said... "give back that beautiful black Cadillac you stole from that wealthy business man with the cards". And...I did. I drove that beautiful black caddy back, over 1000 miles. I tracked the guy down out on the 7th hole of a golf course, signed over the car title to him, gave him the keys and walked away. He was stunned...and...I was Free!

I truly repented "in my heart", and was instantly delivered from my heavy drugs, alcohol and evil, wicked high rolling ways of living.

A true conversion means full repentance from sin.

I have slipped and fallen here and there and not been perfect, but I have repented instantly, wept bitterly, got back up, received my forgiveness, suffered the consequences, but...my choice is "HOLINESS IN CHRIST!" Go and sin no more lest a worse thing come upon you! We reap what we sow. It's one of God's laws.

A Simple Prayer

The day I got saved back in 1974, I prayed a simple prayer, like...Jesus, forgive me. I acknowledge my wickedness. I acknowledge I am suicidal, I acknowledge I need help. I receive you into my heart and life. I repent and turn away from my evil, wicked ways of deception, lies, drunkenness, gambling, drugs and fighting. I will serve you all the days of my life. Deliver me from my self-destruction.

A New Life In The Kingdom Of God

We have already studied Matthew 6:33 where Jesus said; **"Seek first the Kingdom of God AND HIS RIGHTOUSNESS** and all these things (you have need of) will be added unto you".

Step #3

In this final summary I want to briefly deal with...

THE POWER OF RIGHTOUSNESS

Righteousness means **"To be morally right or justifiable"**. It's "right standing with your Heavenly Father". Now, Jesus is our righteousness. But...we must make an "act of the will and choose" to live a righteous life before God and man. Jesus' blood cleanses us from all our unrighteous sinful acts, but this does not mean we go around shooting people, stealing, lying, cheating, committing adultery, a filthy perverted mindset, homosexuality, or any other shameful or violent acts. Here's the point. Choose to live a righteous life. If you fall, get up, receive your forgiveness, go...and sin no more!

- 1 John 3:7 Little children, make sure **no one deceives you**; the one who **practices righteousness** is righteous, just as He (Jesus) is **righteous**.

101

- **Genesis 6:9 These are the records of the generations of Noah. Noah was a righteous man, blameless in his time. Noah walked with God.**

- Noah was also the only one saved in the flood. Him and His family. **Righteousness** is the key to **"WIN THE WAR WITHIN!"**

- **1 Kings 15:11 states; Asa did what was right (righteous) in the sight of the Lord, like David his father.**

- Psalms 32:11 Be glad in the Lord and rejoice you **righteous ones** and shout for joy, all you who are **upright** in heart.

- **Psalms 45:7 You have loved righteousness and hated wickedness. Therefore God, your God, has anointed you with the oil of joy above your fellows.**

- Luke 2:25 And there was a man in Jerusalem whose name was Simeon; and this man was **righteous** and devout, looking for the consolation of Israel; and the Holy Spirit was upon him. (Because he chose to be righteous, "within his heart" toward God).

Notice: The Holy Spirit is where righteousness walks. Jesus is **our righteousness**. He cleanses us from all unrighteousness. But make no mistake. *This is an act of your will to choose to live a Godly, holy, life to the utmost*. To carry on living in my sin and gambling, and stealing all the money at the tables...I would be dead today. It was fun at the time but I knew my life was over if I didn't find an answer. Christ and His Kingdom is the solution to man's "insanity and mental illness problem!" I was suicidal. But not now! Always remember: There's hope and forgiveness...but...don't play with God because you reap what you sow and it can be a bitter pill to swallow if you make foolish, insane choices. Believe me...I know!

Repentance and *righteousness* walk hand in hand. Anything less is rebellion against God. You are maybe going to some church building but you are **not** in God's Kingdom and a part of the body of Christ according to scripture if you willingly carry on in sin when you know right from wrong!

- **2 Corinthians 6:14 Do not be bound together with unbelievers; for what partnership have righteousness and lawlessness, or what fellowship has light with darkness?**

- 2 Timothy 3:15-16 study the sacred writings which are able to give you wisdom that leads to salvation through faith in Christ Jesus. All scripture is inspired by God and profitable for teaching, for reproof, for correction for training in **righteousness**.

- **Matthew 5:6 Blessed are those who hunger and thirst for righteousness, for they shall be satisfied.**

- Psalms 146:8 The Lord opens the eyes of the blind. The Lord raises up those who are bowed down. The Lord loves the **righteous**. (This is an act of the will and the grace of God through Christ to overcome evil with good).

  Righteousness is a choice. Choose to do what is right. God's heart is grieved by all the sin in the "so-called church" today. Lesbian preachers, homosexual preachers, night club rock music performances and flat out abominations **are not righteousness** according to **"GODS HOLY WORD!"** You choose!

- **Proverbs 11:5-6 The righteousness of the blameless will smooth his way, but the wicked will fall by his own wickedness! You choose. We just experienced the horrible Las Vegas murders. This man was either demon possessed or just watched to many murder movies, played to many killer video games or was brain washed by "wrong concepts and wrong choices!" Murder was in his heart! Murder is not right...ousness! "The war is within!" This was pre-meditated murder. His thoughts ruled him! Out of the heart flow the issues of life! Proverbs 4:23**

- Matthew 7:13 Enter through the narrow gates for wide is the gate and broad is the road that leads to destruction and many enter through it.

- **Romans 3:31 Do we then make void God's laws through faith? God forbid; yet we establish the law. (When you break God's laws, his laws break you) You reap what you sow. That's a law! Eg. Break the law of gravity or electricity and you will have a very negative experience! The realm of the spirit within man's heart is exactly the same.**

- John 8:11 Jesus said: To the women caught in adultery "neither do I condemn you: *go, and sin no more"*.
  We can be forgiven for our past but from this day forth...go and sin no more. Willful sin is an act of the will. If you slip and fall that is one thing...but to continue on in your sin when you know the truth...you are in serious danger of hell. You are definitely separated from God's anointing because willful sin separates God and man. Repent and make

things right and God's mercy is there to help you overcome.

- **Romans 2:4 Or do you despise the riches of His goodness, and forbearance, and long suffering for the goodness of God leads you to repentance. (Our God is a good and kind loving merciful God). But don't think you can just accept Christ and continue on in sin like many of these false preachers, active homosexual and lesbian preachers are preaching! They are dead wrong!**

- Matthew 5:20 For I say unto you, that except **your righteousness** shall exceed the **righteousness** of the scribes and Pharisees, *you shall not in no case enter the Kingdom of Heaven.*

  Let these scriptures speak for themselves. This is God's word...not mine. Don't get mad at me I didn't write the Bible, I just follow it. Rebellion is a manifestation of the fallen race of Satan's Kingdom within you.

- **Proverbs 11:4 Riches of this world profit nothing in the day of God's wrath*; but righteousness delivers you from death.***

- Revelation 21:8 But the fearful, and unbelieving, and the abominable, and murderers and whoremongers, and sorcerers, and idolaters and all liars shall have their part in the lake which burns with fire and brimstone: which is the second death. (This is willful unrighteousness!)

- **Matthew 5:8 Blessed are the pure in heart for they shall see God. (For those who don't see God and struggle...repentance, righteousness and** holiness unto the Lord set you FREE). That's the only way... **"TO WIN THE WAR WITHIN!"**

- Matthew 13:41-43 The Son of Man (Christ) will send forth His angels and they will gather out of His Kingdom all stumbling blocks, (anyone trying to block the truth of the gospel of the Kingdom of God) and those who commit lawlessness (sin) and will throw them into the furnace of fire; in that place there will be weeping and gnashing of teeth. Then the **righteous** will shine forth as the sun in the Kingdom of Their Father. He who has ears... **"let him hear!"**

Step #4 – This is One of the "Many Keys" to the Kingdom. I will discuss the other keys in Part 2 of this three-part series.

FORGIVENESS

- **Matthew 6: 14 & 15 For if you forgive men their trespasses your heavenly Father will also forgive you:**

- **15) But if you forgive not men their trespasses, neither will your Father forgive your trespasses.** *This is living and doing God's will...not fake religion!*

Forgive those who have hurt you. Your father, your mother, a relative, business partner, former friend, spouse. Whoever! Forgiveness is a key that unlocks the door "on earth as it is in Heaven" and brings healing "within". This is "How You Win The War Within!"

Step #5 – Find a Good Church or Home Bible Study that preaches the Kingdom of God, and teaches Christ, get plugged in, ask them about water Baptism and get growing in Christ. Get a good King James Bible and study it each day. Start in the Book of John, the Book of LOVE.

This is the "gospel" of the "good news" of the Kingdom of God and His Righteousness! You choose! Choose to walk in Christ, in Holiness, and in His Righteousness. Amen.

What Is My Choice Regarding Eternal Life?

What Will Be My Final Outcome?

What do I Want Others to Say About Me at My Funeral? (This helps you clarify your purpose, vision and mission)

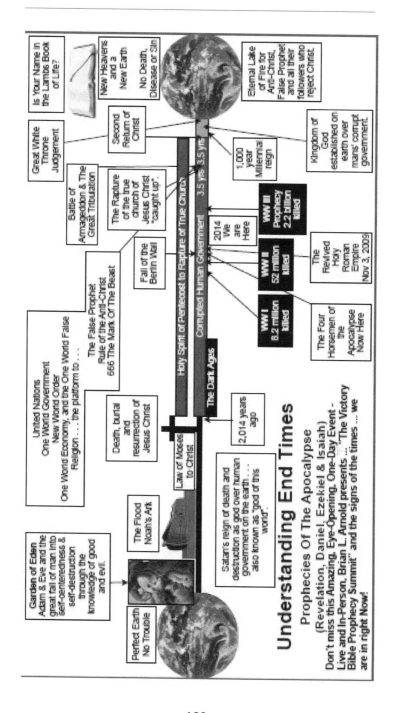

Understanding End Times

Prophecies Of The Apocalypse

(Revelation, Daniel, Ezekiel & Isaiah)

Don't miss this Amazing, Eye-Opening, One-Day Event - Live and In-Person, Brian L Arnold presents ... "The Victory Bible Prophecy Summit" and the signs of the times ... we are in right Now!

Brian's Life Story of How He Was Translated from the Kingdom of Darkness into the Kingdom of Light...Instantly!

We all have a story to tell...here's a small part of mine.

I was born in Winnipeg, Manitoba, Canada in 1950 and raised in the Meadow Lake, Saskatchewan area. Rejected even while in the womb as an illegitimate child, I have never met my father, and I was fortunately adopted within the family (an aunt and uncle adopted me), Olive and Leonard Arnold. My adopted father was a fur trader and bought and sold fish and fur from the natives in northern Saskatchewan during the 40s and 50s. He sold the fur to the Hudson's Bay Co. We had a small mink ranch, sawmill and big, old 3-ton truck to haul fish, fur, lumber and trade goods to our native friends.

When I turned six years old, my father sold everything and bought a little farm so I could go to school. I started my own one-mile trapline at age six. By nine years of age I made enough money trapping to buy a horse and extend my trapline to seven miles. What a happy, wholesome life I had as a young boy!

I left home in 1966 at the age of sixteen to work on the oil rigs in B.C. to help keep our humble little farm. It was still a very difficult time, left over from the 1930's depression. By age nineteen, I was a mess, a drunkard, a womanizer, doing drugs and on the highway to hell ... fast!

Introduced to Card Sharks

One evening, or I should say three o'clock in the morning, I arrived at a "booze can" in Prince George, B.C. and there was a small poker game about to start in the back room. A well-dressed, sophisticated gentleman approached me and pulled me off to the side and said, "How would you like to make $500 in the next hour or two just sitting at the card table?" I said, "Sure! What do I have to do and why me?" He said, "Because you seem pretty sharp kid and we've heard good things about you and we trust you." (I was nicknamed "the kid" from that day on.)

Well, at this point I don't know this man. He's new in town. But soon two or three of my so-called "friends" winked in my direction and said, "It's okay. He's a professional card shark. He'll take all the money, but he will dump it all on you. You'll win it, but he's the one "controlling" the game."

He gave me $500 up front. We started playing at the table and soon I had over $10,000 piled up in front of me in cash and checks. No I.O.U.s ... all from two unsuspecting victims (out of town businessmen) brought to the afterhours club by two hookers. The two girls each got their cut of the action and "bang" I began my journey down the highway to my doom!

This man, I'll call him Mr. Shark, introduced me to Mr. Darkness who in turn introduced me to three or four other highly sophisticated .007 type characters with more heavy connections and money, cars, glitz and glamour, beach cabins, airplanes, wine, women, and song than a young man could ever imagine. I was hooked! I was trapped! I was snared! But I didn't know it yet! These unsuspecting, highly sophisticated, sharks were spread out from Vegas to Alaska.

While this Mr. Shark and Mr. Darkness (both are now dead) were in the city, we had private games every night for two or three weeks. I sat in on each game as the money was spread around each night, cut up after the game and I got my $500 for being the stall man" (the one all the money was dumped onto). Well ... I quit working at the hotel slinging beer, as they wanted me to "go on the road" with them "full time."

They said, "Come with us and we'll show you the ropes of the "good life." The "lazy man's way to riches." We know "what to do" and "how to do it," and we want you to dump "all the money onto," and we want you to protect us if there is ever a fight." (Fortunately, there was only one dangerous fight and it wasn't over gambling, but over a drunk trying to beat up his wife. I narrowly escaped losing my life when the guns came out.) But there was never a fight in all the hundreds and hundreds and hundreds of games I would sit in over the next four "very fast" years of my life.

Soon I had new cars, we had won goldmines in the Yukon, logging companies in British Columbia (and sold them back to the victims), traveled every highway from Alaska to Vegas to Chicago, ate steak and lobster till I was tired of it and stayed in more high class, 5-star resort hotels than the president of the United States. All for what?!

I had been in games at stags where twenty million dollars in cash was on the tables, and armed guards from the mob were protection from robberies. One night, over $500,000.00 (yes, five hundred thousand!) was chopped up 50/50 to the setup guys and us. Many of the games were set up by guys who wore black suits, black hats, dark glasses, packed heavy artillery, smoked big fat cigars and were chauffeured in long black limousines! It was starting to get a little heavy for my liking and like the animals of the forest of my childhood ... I could smell it and sense trouble. I was going deeper and deeper into the pit of hell and it was getting too hot for me ... .

I Wanted Out!

But how do you get out? When I was a young trapper and set snares ... the snared animal never got out. The animal wanted to. It tried, it struggled! It fought! But the animal rarely if ever escaped my traps. Now … I, the little trapper boy, was trapped … in a prison of my own making.

After going through millions of dollars in gambling … I was still empty inside. There seemed like a great empty hole in my soul that no drug, alcohol, gambling money, positive thinking or person could fill. I had tried it all. I had drifted so far from my down-to-earth reality, and great clouds of depression were beginning to gather round about me. It seemed as though I had gained the whole world of "money" and "things," but I had lost myself. I could hear this faint little cry, deep down in the dark dungeon of my heart, crying for freedom, but I could see no light. I felt as though I were one of the living dead. I was empty. Empty, empty, empty!

I had many questions arising now in my heart about life. Who am I? Why am I here? Is this all there is to life" What's my purpose for being here? What is life? Is life worth living any longer"? Depression was setting in deeper, so I drank more, smoked more pot, did more drugs and spiraled deeper into the bottomless pit of despair. I was searching for answers. but I was asking the wrong questions to all the wrong people. Demons began to whisper "suicide" into my ear, and confusion increased. I was lost - a high-rolling gambling drunk; void. empty inside, and without hope.

Finally, at the age of twenty-four like a prodigal son, worn out, wrung out and with a large, dark ball and chains of drugs, alcohol and gambling clamped to my life of destruction, corruption and death, I made my weary way back home hoping to buy my Mother and Father's farm and try to find peace within my soul. I was spiritually dead, but didn't know it. I had everything outwardly the world could offer, but . . . I was dead inside.

So, I bought my Mother and Father's farm from my heavily-laden pockets filled with all my ill-gotten-gain. The little farm I had slaved over as a young boy, but oh what a simple, quiet, and warm welcome to my troubled, sick, and very heavy self-centered heart. I bought the farm, with some of my ill-gotten cash. Mom and Dad moved into town and soon I expanded the farm; bought more land, larger equipment, more cattle, and a new pick-up. All was great! Except for one problem. I couldn't shake the dark depression and strong urges at times, of ending my life. Outwardly I now had a nice farm. To those around me ... everything looked good. In town they would ask me on the street, "How are you doing, Brian?" I would answer, "Great!" But it was a lie. I was living a lie. Inwardly I had nothing! I had no life! No purpose. No reason for living. I had lots of questions about life, but no one could answer them. Depression had grown from a whisper of "suicide" in my ear into an uncontrollable roaring 500-pound gorilla and I couldn't figure out where it had come from, nor how to shake it off my back. It was fast becoming a roaring headless monster.

A prideful arrogant, self-centered, egotistical, tough guy was now looking back at me from the mirror and I did not like who I saw. But what could the inner, snared little trapper boy do with this shameful, empty man staring back from the glass. Take his life? I thought death might be a relief, but yet I felt there had to be more to life than all this "stuff," for I had it all and yet I had nothing. I felt like zero inside. An EMPTY zero inside. I had lots outwardly ... yet nothing inwardly except pride, arrogance and a self-centered ego. I had a war of "good" and "evil" going on inside of me and it seemed that evil was winning.

I remember very clearly the day I was sitting on the ladder leaning up against our old barn and a gathering of demon spirits attacking me, "Suicide! Suicide! End it all now. Go to the garage. Get your gun and end it." So, I headed for the garage to get my gun and end my life. Fortunately, a neighbor drove into the yard at that moment and I didn't follow through with their dark evil suggestions at that time. I wrestled with these dark thoughts, feelings, and demons for another week or so.

Finally, I decided to go to church and go to Mom and Dad's afterwards for lunch. I remember that day so well. It was July of 1974. I got up, it was a beautiful summer morning. I was preparing to go to Mass (the first time in 8 years) and ... about 50 head of my cows somehow got out of the fence and were on the road.

So, I quickly rounded them up, fixed the fence, changed clothes and sped off to town to hopefully get to Mass on time. But I was late. Mass started at 9:30 AM and it was 9:45 AM. I hate being late for "any" appointment or meeting. Of course, I didn't really care if I went to Mass or not, because I was not a "religious person" but I knew of "spiritual activity" because of the pow-wows with my dad, and our native friends were very spiritually attuned to calling and contacting "spirits." So, I was somewhat spiritually attuned, but not religiously inclined.

So, because I was late I decided not to go to Mass, even though I saw my Mom and Dad's car at the church. I decided to go to their house and sit around, have a coffee and wait until they got home.

A Divine Appointment

As I was driving to my parent's home I remember distinctly stopping at the stop sign in front of the police station in Meadow Lake, Saskatchewan. And . . . an old school chum, Richard Pliska came walking right in front of my pick-up truck.

We recognized each other. Richard asked me, "What are you doing Brian?" and I said, "I was going to go to Mass, but I'm late, so I'm just going to my parent's house." He said, "Well, our church starts in just 10 minutes, why not come and join us?" Well ... what could I say?

Now, dear reader, you must clearly understand here at this point, I was raised Roman Catholic. I was even indoctrinated as an "altar boy." I was told and taught that Roman Catholics are the "only ones" going to heaven. I was told that Christ died for our sins, but "it was the Virgin Mary who would pray us through." Or, if I died I would at least "go to purgatory" and "if someone paid enough money for enough masses I could be prayed out of purgatory into heaven."

I had no concept of "true" spiritual realities or biblical truths at this point, other than traditional native pow-wows with my native brothers contacting spirits or go to Mass, pay your money, confess your sins to some priest in a black robe, say "Our Fathers", "ten Hail Mary's" on the rosary for penance and so on and so forth. It was all ritual, Latin and form, but ... I was Roman Catholic. I was taught that if I was "baptized" ... that's all that was needed. It was my traditional upbringing and we were taught we were the "only ones" going to heaven. Period. So, for me to suddenly go into a little "Gospel" Church across the street was out of the question! The thought had never crossed my mind. I had heard stories of these nut cases, holy roller fanatics, and I wanted no part of it. But Richard was such a kind young man. He gently suggested again that I join him because they had a "special speaker," a black man from America.

I thought, "What is a black preacher from America doing in a rinky-dink little church in a rinky-dink little town in northern Saskatchewan?" I was curious. So, with cautious reluctance and fair warning to my friend, that if anything funny started going on I'd punch the first guy out that got in my face and level everybody else around me ... real quick! I walked in with him. (When I look back now, what a pathetic state of mind I had grown into. This is a sure sign of a wicked heart of anger, mistrust, self-centeredness, and fear.)

Anyway, Richard and I went into this little "Bible-preaching" Gospel Church of perhaps 30 - 40 people at 9:55 AM on this beautiful summer Sunday morning. However, I was ill prepared for what was about to happen. We had to sit up closer to the front, as the back pews were all filled and you didn't dare sit in Momma Bear or Papa Bear's pew. So we found our place and sat down. A few others came in after us and sat beside us on both sides, and "I" was stuck in the middle.

But, I'm tough and not afraid of anything. I'm super macho. I've gone where supposedly angels fear to tread, where guns were at private games and armed guards watched the doors as tens of thousands of dollars changed hands. So, why would I be nervous around a bunch of nice smiling innocent, God-fearing people?

But something was different here. I sensed it quickly, but I didn't know what it was. They played their guitars, sang 5 or 6 songs, a few old hymns, made a few announcements, and then invited their "guest speaker" to share "God's Holy Word" with us. It was all very different for me, compared to my Roman Catholic upbringing.

Now remember, me being a Roman Catholic (though I was wretched to the core), as long as you confessed your sins to the priest, did your penance and followed all the traditional forms, you were supposedly okay. You could go back and curse God on Monday and live like the devil, commit adultery, get drunk, go to the bingo games in the church, gamble, but be at Mass on Sunday to Confess your sins again. Hypocritical, but that's the way it was.

Well, when this dear, old black man got up to speak he brought fire down from Heaven. It was as if he hurled lightning rods and thunderbolts out into that little audience ... but God was speaking TO ME through him. He was a fireball, full of the power of Almighty God, and the power and conviction of the words that flowed from his inner-most

117

being jolted me to the very core of my being. It was from spirit to spirit. Not head to head. Big difference! I had never heard of such things. I was used to a bit of talk by a priest along with some very religious sounding and pious looking traditions and forms of godliness, but it had "no power." It sounded "reverent" and looked pious but it was "powerless" and without conviction. It was plastic religion.

This guy had power! God's Holy Spirit Power! It was real! He was speaking from his heart with great conviction. You have to realize dear reader, that in the past eight years before listening to this preacher, that I had been schooled in the fine art of "reading people." I could tell if you had money or no money, all bluff or if you had the goods. I was taught by "the best" and had a refined PhD in street smarts.

I was reading this guy like a hawk watching a rabbit, but I was "no match" for the Power of God that was flowing out of his heart and nailing me right between the eyes. I was stunned, elated, fired full of hope and in wonderment at why no one had ever shared this message of the Power and Glory, Deliverance, and Hope of the Lord Jesus Christ and Him crucified! I had never heard of such reality, such power, such hope, such DELIVERANCE, such care LOVE and MERCY for a wretched sinner full of emptiness, hopelessness, selfishness, and despair such as I.

This dear little, old black man was sent by God to deliver me from my wretchedness, guilt, greed, and despair. God had heard my cry, and he hears yours and has sent you this little article to DELIVER YOU out of your prison of despair, loneliness, emptiness, and self-centeredness. He did it that day for me and he'll do it for you right now, if you don't harden your heart against God's love and delivering power.

He declared that the Holy Bible states, "all liars, thieves, drunkards, murderers, homosexuals, adulterers, idolaters and sorcerers would spend eternity in the lake of fire and brimstone if they didn't repent from their sin and get saved!" He fired out how, "In the days of old, corruption, filthy perverted evil thoughts and violence filled men's hearts and God sent a flood, saving only Noah, his family and two of every creature in the Ark." He declared how, "Sodom and Gomorrah were perverted in homosexuality and He turned those cities into salt and brimstone because of their rebellion." He declared how, "Jesus' second return is close at hand and the entire earth will be consumed in fire in the final judgment, and that today Jesus Christ is the "ark of protection" and is coming back real soon!"

This shook me to the core as his piercing eyes looked through my darkened soul, as he fired out, "You must be "BORN AGAIN" to be forgiven and delivered from your sin!" I thought, "What do you mean, born again?" I had never heard of such a thing. He shared how, "In the beginning God created the Heavens and the Earth by the Word of His Power. He spoke it into existence." God said, "Let there be light and it shot out at 186,000 miles per second and is still travelling throughout the universe at that speed. He called the light day and darkness night."

We Are Creative Spirit Beings

The difference between man and animals is . . . animals have the instinct to survive. Man . . . like his Creator . . . has the ability to create. We are creative spirit beings. Most dis-eases and most dis-orders are not "caught" but are "created" within.

This preacher-man talked about God creating man in His Image and Likeness, a "creative spirit being" with a self Image. How he formed Adam from the dust of the ground and breathed the "breath of Life" into him and he became a God-centered living soul and how Adam and Eve disobeyed God in the Garden of Eden and had a tragic fall. Not forward, not backward, but inward ... into SELF-

119

centeredness, from God-centeredness and consequently missed the mark of their high calling.

And "missing of the mark" became known as "sin" or a rebellious lawbreaker of God's universal laws. Because of this ... the taint of sin and the curse of self-destruction is in the bloodline of all humanity, passed on from generation to generation, originating from our very first parents - Adam and Eve.

That's why universal man is now under the curse of alcoholism, lying, cheating, stealing, perversion, promiscuity and corruption, because it's "in their blood." And that curse is passed on from generation to generation from Adam and Eve down. (Not from monkeys, polliwog soup, and evolution!) What a lying deception from the pit of hell and the spirit of anti (against) Christ, Satan himself.

As the power and "anointing" of God's Holy Spirit, and the Fire of All-mighty God began to fall upon me under the sound of this man's voice, I began to shudder as the Spirit of God shed light on my darkened heart. I wasn't just sick in the head, but sick in the heart, my self-centered "inner spirit man" (what psychologists, psychiatrists, and humanism call the great powers of the "sub- conscious mind"). Out of the heart ("inner spirit man") flow the "issues of life"!

Like hot coals off the altar of God, his words melted my hardened heart and I was gripped, arrested, and in awe of the reality with which this man spoke. I thought, "Who told this man of my wretchedness? How does he know I am so rotten to the core? But Richard could not have, he has been here with me all the time. No one else here even knows me." But ... GOD KNEW ME. He knows each one of us in our spirit. And ... He was speaking to me in my spirit by His Holy Spirit through the spirit of this little, black preacher.

I was dumbfounded, jolted, perplexed, and as it were ... a spiritually dead man sitting in my body. I began to shake inwardly as my spirit cried out "This is it! This is what I've been searching for all my life! It's deliverance, and salvation and it has come at last!" It's eternal life! It's Truth! This is not phony, plastic, artificial, half-truth, man-made false religion. Finally someone is telling me the Truth! The Truth was setting me free in my spirit from my slavery to all my addictions of lust, gambling, drugs, and alcohol. I, who had been snared by the Enemy Trapper (Satan/Lucifer) of my soul was being set FREE! FREE! by God Almighty through Jesus CHRIST. FINALLY ... the answers to all my questions about life were being answered ... and they made good sense!

The Way, Truth and Life

In closing, the little, black preacher declared that Jesus said, "I am the way, the truth and the life and no one comes to the Father but through me," He declared, "God had laid all the sins of the world, yours and mine, upon an innocent perfect man, Jesus Christ." That He became the sacrificial Lamb (the Substitute, the one and only Mediator between God and man) that was slain for all humanity's sins. He died, was buried. He descended into hell for 3 days of suffering in our place, and on the third day, God said "enough, the price for the world's sin has been paid in full!" He raised Jesus from the dead. Jesus was born again "spiritually" in the depths of hell, ascended into heaven, presented His blood to His Heavenly Father ... God, "the perfect sacrifice," for all of humanity to be DELIVERED. He then returned to earth and appeared to His followers for forty more days." The little preacher declared, "Life is in the blood. So is death! Sin is a blood poisoner! It results in self-destruction, fear, worry, rebellion, and corruption. That's why we need God's Son, Jesus Christ, for there was no sin taint in His bloodline when shed on the cross for our forgiveness. Because God was His Father and the bloodline always flows from the father!"

I was deeply convicted and moved by all that I was hearing. The little, black preacher said, "Jesus died to "reconnect" you back to God. He loves the sinner, but hates the sin." He declared, "Jesus is standing at the door of your heart and wants to come into your life and live with you through His Holy Spirit of Love. He wants to fill you with his Holy Spirit, so you won't be controlled by Satan, the god of this world, and his evil spirits of greed. control, bitterness, jealousy, deceit, envy, pride. and rebellion. You can either call upon Christ and be saved or you are a slave to the curse upon self and Satan, the author of selfishness and headed for hell without a divine intervention."

All Choices Have Consequences!

The little black preacher man declared . . . "You've got to serve somebody! God or Satan. Love or selfishness. Whom do you choose ... this day? The Bible ... "God's Holy Word" ... is "God's Will." A sharp line is drawn between good and evil, light and darkness, life and death, children of God and children of false religions and Satan, the righteous and the wicked, wheat, and chaff, saved and lost, not condemned and condemned already, heaven and hell, selfishness and love ... sharp contrasts with no grey compromises." He declared, "The distinction is summed up in two terms packed with meaning. You are either "in Christ" or you are "in sin and anti-Christ." There is no other!

And ... you have a choice to make. What you choose ... you get! Light or darkness. Good or evil. Heaven or hell. "He fired out that God's holiness and Satan's evil must ... "inevitably must" ... be separated for they cannot live together throughout eternity and the place prepared for all whose choice is to reject Jesus Christ, God's provision, and choose to go their own rebellious way, choose to be anti-Christ and ... choose hell. To choose darkness is to choose future defeat and destruction because the whole world lies in the power of Satan, the evil one. There is no purgatory. It's a lie from Satan and the pit of hell! There is no third place or second chance. God's Word declares it so! Choose now! whom you will serve."

The little, black preacher asked, "Is there anyone here today who would like to be "born again" by accepting Jesus Christ as their Savior and Lord, renounce Satan and his dark evil forces of influence, repent from their sin and begin a "new life" in Christ? A new beginning. A new slate. A new start. Old things will pass away and all things will become new."

"If you would like this, I invite you to come up here to this altar, surrender your life to Jesus Christ and I will pray with you a simple little prayer."

Instantly, I jumped to my feet! Because there were people on each side of me, I stepped over the pew directly in front of me in my blue sports jacket, blue jeans and cowboy boots and I walked straight up to the little, black preacher at the altar. No one else came up and I didn't care. I thought, "only dummies will go to hell and anyone with half-an-ounce of brains will get saved!" I looked him straight in the eye and I said. "Mister ... if this Jesus you're talking about is really real ... I want him and I want him right now!" Well. we bowed our heads and I asked God to forgive me and accepted Jesus Christ, the Prince of Peace. to come into my heart. Instantly, I felt a flash as of lightning and I was translated from darkness to light and the spirit of suicide and death departed ... never to return! I was instantly "born again spiritually" . . .the Greatest Miracle of all! It's Eternal Life.

I began to hear sobs in the sanctuary behind me. Another child had come home; the "little trapper boy" had truly "come home." Because of Jesus Christ, I was introduced FINALLY ... to my Heavenly Father. Creator of the heavens and the earth and now He would be my new

Spiritual Guide, Deliverer. Healer, and Comforter in times of trouble. I was a (0) zero. I was empty inside. Lost and without hope, but that day I made the decision to stop rebelling and leave my street life of crime, addictions, sinfulness and rebellion behind and join with Number (1) One ... Jesus CHRIST and that made me a (10) TEN! I was delivered from half-truth man-made false "religion" and now gained a "relationship" with my Heavenly Father through Jesus Christ--now my personal savior. Jesus had paid the price in full and I accepted it.

That 500-pound gorilla of depression flew off my back like a shot and I've never seen him since. I lit up like a light bulb. I was instantly translated from the Kingdom of Darkness and depression into the Kingdom of Light by the miracle working power of Almighty God, now my Heavenly Father because of Jesus Christ. He filled me with His love and washed away all my sins: guilt, anger, rebellion, resentments and set me FREE. My deck of cards went into the garbage can. I was a free man! I actually felt real love for others in my heart from that moment on. Now, for over forty (1974 - 2014) years, I have walked in total freedom from the cards and any form of gambling. I'm not perfect, but Jesus is. And I'm forgiven. I walk now in true victory over lust, depression, anger, bitterness, envy and jealousy.

Temptations have come and gone. But I broke away from my old influences, stayed away from temptations, and today, more than ever, I walk in the overcoming power of All-Mighty God to these beggarly get-rich-quick, gambling schemes of this world's deceptive systems. I'm a Free Man! I had been delivered from the kingdom of darkness and Satan's grip on my life of slavery, handcuffs, bondages and shackles to addictions and I had been translated into the kingdom of light by the shed blood of Jesus Christ. I was forgiven!

Through Jesus delivered from the kingdom of darkness and Satan's grip on my life of slavery, handcuffs, bondages and shackles to addictions and I had been translated into the kingdom of light by the shed blood of Jesus Christ. I was forgiven! Through Jesus Christ. I was born again! I, who had been spiritually dead in my trespasses and sin. My spirit that had been dead in fear, anxiety, sin, depression, self-destruction, and without hope was now alive, renewed and filled with God's love. Now I can freely, truly, love others! When I surrendered my self-centered will and life to Jesus Christ at the foot of the Cross of Calvary, I was "born again" by the spirit of the living God. God's Spirit of light, life, and love came in and I was delivered and set Free ... Instantly! I have never picked up the cards for a game since.

No man-made tradition, psychologist, psychiatrist, club, philosophy, secret society, man-made half-truth, religion, superstition, false god, cult, occult, false hope, false belief or spiritual entity can perform this miracle of salvation from sin, sickness and demons ... only JESUS CHRIST. Salvation means "Forgiveness from sin" and "deliverance from evil" and brings wholeness, healing, and overcoming power to your entire being ... spirit, soul, and body. This is not "religion" or self-righteousness but a "relationship" with your Heavenly Father ... God ... through Jesus Christ. It is a supernatural revelation of Jesus Christ and His resurrection power!

If you desire physical, mental, emotional or inner healing ... Jesus Christ is God's provision for your inner peace and deliverance right now! He is man's only hope.

So ... dear reader ... do you choose Jesus Christ today for your Salvation ... or do you choose your own rebellious way and fully accept the consequences of eternal separation from your Creator ... God ... throughout eternity? It's a lie of deception from Satan that there are many roads to God - there is only ONE WAY and Jesus Christ is that WAY - or God is a liar, and Jesus Christ died in vain!

Here's a suggested prayer, Oh God, I acknowledge I am a Sinner and in need of a savior. I accept Jesus Christ as my Savior. I understand you (Jesus) are my only way to have all my sins removed. Your pure and righteous blood is my substitute for the sinfulness and unrighteousness of my blood. Upon accepting you, Jesus, I am divorced from my sin and now married into your righteousness. God now accepts me once and for all ... because of you.

I am now "BORN AGAIN" in the "spiritual" sense ... because of you, Jesus. Thank you.

82712989R00070

Made in the USA
Columbia, SC
05 December 2017